Be

Beyond Easter

———— ✦ ————

Through grief to growth

MARTYN DAY

TRIANGLE

First published in Great Britain in 1997
Triangle
SPCK
Holy Trinity Church
Marylebone Road
London NW1 4DU

British Library Cataloguing-in-Publication Data
A catalogue record of this book is available from the British Library

ISBN 0-281-05097-X

Typeset by Mews Photosetting
Printed in Great Britain by
Caledonian International, Glasgow

This book is dedicated to all those
who have helped me see
that to live in the light of Easter
is the only real way to live.

Contents

꘏꘎꘎ꗠ꘎꘎꘏

Acknowledgements

This book would never have been completed, save for the support and encouragement of many. I salute all those who have helped me in this venture, and in particular, the following gallery of people who deserve special mention.

J. John – it was your preaching on the significance of Easter which cemented my faith. I will always be grateful for your commitment to preach the Gospel. Many thanks for encouragements down the years and for your help on this project. You have wielded a sharp and wise editing pen, and crafted a great Foreword. Thank you.

Doreen Middleweek – for being such a wise and encouraging instructor in New Testament Greek. I trust I have been a good student.

The Sheldon family: Steve, Fi, Kate, Tom and Hannah – many thanks for a warm and welcoming home in which one of these chapters was written. Special thanks to Tom for useful information gleaned from the computer. Thanks to you all as well for helping me discover my allergy to rabbits.

For Nottingham friends: Liz and Peter, Claire and Jonathan, Lynn and Val, Steve and Laura – for being so willing to use this material as individuals and as a group. I appreciate your help so much. I have enjoyed some great times of fellowship with you all. Special mention to Iain and Carol, who helped in using the material and, by offering themselves for full-time missionary service, have found the Lord leading them beyond Easter in a very special way.

Rambir Bamra — a faithful friend. Thank you for all your comments, prayers and encouragements. You and the family have a special place in my heart.

My family — thank you for all your love and support down the years.

Honor — my precious wife. Thank you for believing in me and giving lots of space and encouragement in this project. Thank you for the time you have taken to comment on the manuscript. Your perspectives are always insightful. Remember that the early fig is just a sign of future fruitfulness.

The Lord Jesus Christ — no words of praise written here will ever be sufficient to express your merit. All this has been attempted for you and is an expression of my gratitude for the way in which you have taken me beyond Easter.

I am also grateful to Kingsway's Thankyou Music, PO Box 75, Eastbourne, East Sussex BN23 6NT, for permission to use material on pages 39, 62 and 143.

Foreword

꧁꧂

Perhaps it is because of our anticipation of what is promised, that we tend to move too quickly from Easter to Pentecost. Perhaps it is our inability to live with the evidence of what we did to the scarred, wounded Man, that we quickly have him exalted in heaven. Perhaps it is that we long for the time of the miracles and mighty acts of the Spirit and have forgotten that first we need to be patiently taught by Jesus. For whatever reasons, I for one have not been led to think of the time between Easter and the Ascension as a pivotal and formulative time. But I think I need to reassess that in the light of this book.

The light of this book is indeed the Resurrection light, shining from the empty tomb. Martyn Day leads us to see everything in the light which is cast on the world, full of the agony and pain of the crucifixion, by the risen Jesus. We are neither to pretend that this world of suffering and death does not go on around us, nor are we to live in this world as if this is the only reality. I believe that the focus of this book will keep us from such escapism or defeatism; rather, we learn that, although we live in a world which crucified the Messiah and Saviour, yet this same one comes to journey with us, to lead us to the place where he is. Or, as Martyn says, 'there is nowhere he will ask us to go without going before us to prepare the way.'

I hope that, like me, you will be drawn deeper into each of these stories, as Martyn redraws pictures we thought we knew, in such a different way, that you wonder why you didn't see things before which are now visible. There is such a depth of perception and imagination which open up these Easter stories. This book invites us to become part of the narrative: to be at the tomb and realize we do not have to move the stone for ourselves; to stand with Mary at the tomb and hear Jesus call us by name and wipe away our tears; to walk along the Emmaus Road which is full of our disappointments and lack of understanding, and feel our hearts burn within us as Jesus comes alongside; to stand with Thomas in his doubts to receive an invitation to fresh trust; to feel the weight of Peter's denials and the joy of once again hearing the call; we are enticed into being one of the disciples confronted by the Author of Life who speaks into shattered lives, characterized by fear and hopelessness.

For these stories are part of our inheritance. They are in some extraordinary way our stories. The more we enter into them, the more we will find them to be truth-telling about God, about us and about our life together. For the first disciples, the reality of the crucifixion made life unliveable. Many of us also struggle with life today. If Good Friday has the last word, if indeed God is dead, the world and our lives are hopelessly meaningless. But if he is risen and alive, all is changed.

To take these stories to heart is to begin to live with the startling, transforming presence of the risen Jesus, to try and cope with the newness of Easter. It is to live in the world which is the place of crucifixion and death, but a world invaded by the new heavenly light of the risen Jesus. He deals with our past and opens up the future in a way that previously would be unimaginable. He resets our horizons and leads us forward.

I hope and pray that Martyn's book will be to you a re-orientation. It is full of poignant advice and true facing of the questions which deeply reside in our lives. There are practical prayers and a profound interweaving of these stories with our own everyday experience. There is much to think on throughout the whole day. I hope and pray that in this book you are captured again by the risen Jesus and that you are able, in a more profound and freeing way than ever, to throw yourself into the arms of God and the hands of the Saviour, which bear the marks of his commitment to us, but carry us to glory.

J. John

Prologue

In my former book, Theophilus, I wrote about all that Jesus began to do and to teach until the day he was taken up to heaven, after giving instructions through the Holy Spirit to the apostles he had chosen. After his sufferings, he showed himself to these men and gave many convincing proofs that he was alive. He appeared to them over a period of forty days and spoke about the Kingdom of God.

(Acts 1.1-3)

The period between the resurrection of Jesus and his ascension has tended to be eclipsed by our concentration on the season of Lent. Our preparations for Easter are important, but the truths of the resurrection need to sink deep within us and take root in the days which follow Easter. Unlike Lent, the 40-day period after Easter Day carries no special name-tag, and no particular traditions are associated with it. It is possible, therefore, for this period to become a forgotten phase in the life of the Church.

And yet for the first disciples of Jesus, this was a crucial time of transition. A ragged band of men and women, scattered and scared by the horrifying events of Good Friday, are moulded together into the very beginnings of the Church. Their doubts are dispelled, their fears are dissolved and a new-found confidence is implanted which drives them outwards in missionary zeal. What a transformation!

Those disciples had to wrestle with the implications of a risen Jesus, who had conquered death and was about to bestow on them the gift of the Holy Spirit. They entered this post-Easter period with a tangled mass of emotions. Some were torn inside by grief, others had seen long-cherished dreams fizzle into nothing. There were those who carried guilt and remorse, and all were fearful of the future. Questions and reproaches galore must have preyed on their minds:

'If only I had …?'
'What if …?'
'Why didn't I …?'
'How could this have been?'

Into this confused gathering, the risen Jesus comes. It is interesting that in his prologue to the book of Acts, Luke does not mention that Jesus performed any miracles during this post-Easter period. In many ways, the first disciples had quite enough to cope with trying to come to terms with the miracle of his resurrection. What Luke does record is that Jesus' main focus at this time was on *teaching* his disciples. It was a time of reflection, training and finally of sending out with the task of spreading his good news to all nations (the great commission, as it's been called, given in Matthew 28. 19–20).

In this book we will follow the journey of these first disciples, from the dawn of that first Easter morning, to the day on the Mount of Olives when they witnessed the ascension, having received the great commission to spread the good news about him. As we remember their thoughts and feelings, their doubts and struggles, and witness how the risen Christ led them on, let us too meet with him, and allow the truths of Easter to take root within us. Let us hear his call and be equipped and encouraged to respond to Jesus' call to action.

The 40 readings from the Gospels and Acts follow chronologically the events of this post-Easter period. For each day there are some thoughts for reflection and some questions to help you apply the truths of Scripture to your own life. The readings are grouped into sections relating to each of Jesus' resurrection appearances. Each section opens with the Bible passage recounting the appearance. Hold these verses in your mind throughout the time you spend with each section. You may like to reread the opening passage each day if you have time. Each day begins with a specific verse to focus the thoughts, and ends with a prayer. The final section of the book contains some outlines for group work on post-Easter themes.

Our time with the Lord is among the most precious moments of each day. In writing this book I have been aware of the responsibility of sharing truths from Scripture. I have not taken this responsibility lightly. I am grateful to you for choosing to spend some of your time with the Lord in the company of these readings. I pray you will find the book helpful.

Jesus led his first disciples on a journey from confusion to commission. As he takes us beyond Easter, may he lead us on that same journey, with his light consuming our darkness, and his Holy Spirit equipping us to shine with that light, serving him with renewed strength and passion.

Contemplating the Empty Tomb

On the first day of the week, very early in the morning, the women took the spices they had prepared and went to the tomb.

(Luke 24.1)

And they asked each other, 'Who will roll the stone away from the entrance to the tomb?' But when they looked up, they saw that the stone, which was very large, had been rolled away.

(Mark 16.3–4)

While they were wondering about this, suddenly two men in clothes that gleamed like lightning stood beside them.

(Luke 24.4)

'Do not be afraid, for I know that you are looking for Jesus, who was crucified.'

(Matthew 28.5)

'Why do you look for the living among the dead? He is not here; he has risen! Remember how he told you, while he was still with you in Galilee, "The Son of Man must be delivered into the hands of sinful men, be crucified and on the third day be raised again."' Then they remembered his words. When they came back from the tomb, they told all these things to the Eleven and to all the others. But they did not believe the women, because their words seemed like nonsense.

(Luke 24.5–9, 11)

Day 1 (Easter Day)

The God with another chapter up his sleeve

The Christ will suffer and rise from the dead on the third day.

(Luke 24.46)

It was no ordinary morning. While most of Jerusalem slept, a small group of women made their way through the darkness to the garden tomb of their master. It is surprising to have recorded in such detail a visit to a burial place. Countless visits have been made to tombs, graves and other resting places all over the world. We would be hard pressed to find many of these visits documented. Why this one? We, with the benefit of hindsight, know the whole story of Easter – but the women did not have this advantage. No, it was certainly no ordinary morning. It was the most important morning in the history of the world. The morning to begin all mornings. The morning whose very dawning was to herald a new era of hope. The beginning of that day was to usher in a succession of new beginnings for men, women and children in every generation. Jesus was alive!

But those women did not know what they were to discover. For them, it was their last act of devotion. A closing of the chapter. The end of their hopes, dreams and ideals. They were writing the end of the Jesus story. It would have been a fitting way to wrap up the tale, except that God had begun another chapter before the women had had a chance to finish theirs. God's intervention was to rekindle hopes, fulfil dreams and restore ideals.

How often do we encounter a situation and believe it to be the final outcome? Easter teaches us that God's plans are never thwarted by the full-stop which we ourselves place at the end of a chapter in our lives. Yet so often our own actions can deny him the opportunity to have the final say. Surely God's final word is best. We may write, 'The End'; God may have planned a sequel. We may close the book; God may just turn the page. For all we know, our lives may include some chapters that God has only just begun. And the only thing which will stop us reaching the ending he has for us is our own decision to settle for an outcome which falls short of this.

It is ironic that of all the people in the Gospels, the Pharisees were the only group who acted with any kind of expectation that Jesus might rise from the dead. While the Jews persuaded Pilate to seal up the tomb, the disciples sealed themselves up in the upper room. The women were preparing spices for Jesus whom they believed was dead; the Pharisees were setting defences just in case Jesus came alive. The early disciples were clearly not expecting Jesus to rise from the dead, despite all he himself had said to this effect and despite the Messianic prophecies from the Old Testament which also foretold it. God's next chapter in the Jesus story had been written, but not appreciated; studied throughout the generations, but not understood.

And God is writing new chapters for us, too. God is never left speechless or helpless. His creativity extends to us on all levels. The God who sprinkled the heavens with the constellations is the same God who, in Jesus, bent to write in the dust of the earth before the woman caught in adultery (John 8.6–8). God's creativity never runs dry.

Easter, and the days which follow, are a wonderful opportunity to discover another chapter which God has written for us. We may feel at a dead-end in some areas in our lives. God does not intend us to set up camp there and make a home for ourselves. He can show us a way out to fulfilment and purpose.

So today, let us celebrate the God who takes our story on and can breathe fresh life into what may seem a flagging narrative. For the power which raised Christ from the

3

dead is at work in us to bring us to maturity in him. Happy Easter.

For further reflection

1 Think about other instances in the Bible, in your own life and in the lives of people you know when God has brought a fresh breath of life into a situation in which there seemed to be no hope. Give thanks for each instance you can think of. Praise him that he is the God of new beginnings.

2 Think about any areas in your life which you feel are dead-ends, where you have drawn a finishing line. Offer these areas to the Lord at the start of this 40-day journey, and ask him to show you during these days if there is anything new that he wants to do in these areas of your life.

A prayer

Lord, thank you for Easter Day,
For the hope of fresh starts and new beginnings.
I praise you that you are risen from the dead
and active in my life today,
by the same power that raised you from the dead.
Breathe fresh life into these days to come
that I may be alive with your life
and filled with your power
to display your glory.
In Jesus' name. Amen.

Day 2 (Monday)

※

Questions in the darkness

'Who will roll the stone away from the entrance to the tomb?'

(Mark 16.3)

We will be spending the next seven days contemplating more closely those first moments surrounding the discovery of the empty tomb. There is such an enormous feast of human experience in this brief incident that we would do well to pause and savour it in small portions. Spending so much time on one story may be a new experience. My prayer is that new insights will be given as we view this event from different angles.

We saw yesterday how the women came to the tomb unprepared to find it empty. They fully expected to find Jesus' dead body, and were bringing spices to anoint it. They came that morning, not primarily through obedience to the Jewish customs of burial, but more out of love for Jesus. It was devotion, not duty, that took them. But they came, too, with hidden questions about all that had happened. John's Gospel reminds us that it was still dark when the women first set out for the tomb (John 20.1). And as the early sunshine begins to pierce the dawn, Mark reveals one of the questions which preyed on the minds of the women: '"Who will roll the stone away from the entrance to the tomb?"' (Mark 16.3). It was a simple and straightforward question which, interestingly, is recorded only by Mark, for it is he who emphasizes the large size of the stone itself (Mark 16.4).

The women were well aware that the stone was a real barrier between them and the respect they wished to pay to Jesus' body by anointing it. They appear to have had no firm ideas for moving the stone. Their devotion to Jesus overrode all other issues. I can imagine them busily preparing spices on Good Friday evening, without thinking about the practicalities of getting past the stone. And then, on their way to the tomb, the realization hits them as clearly as the dawn breaks around them – the stone! How will they move the stone? It would have been far too heavy for them to move by themselves – and it was also sealed by the Romans and there were guards to deal with.

Isn't it like that for us sometimes, when we discover issues in our lives which we have not always recognized until something particular triggers them off? We can spend weeks, months, maybe years, hedging around issues and not facing them … until one day when they come face to face with us unmistakably.

Until recently I couldn't swim. Some unfortunate childhood experiences had given me a fear of water which had always kept me from learning. It was an issue which was always there, but one which I had always been able to avoid: I could choose not to let it impinge too much on my life. All that changed when I met Honor (who is now my wife). She enjoyed swimming, and I was often left to stand on the side watching her. Realizing that this could be something we could share, I resolved to learn to swim. It wasn't easy, and I believe that my own prayers and those of others enabled me to face my fear of water and begin to enjoy swimming. I cannot say I am completely water-safe, but I have in many ways faced a long-standing problem and, with God's help, found a way of resolving it.

The women knew they were going to come face to face with the issue of the tombstone. They had also begun to realize that in themselves they were incapable of solving the problem. Assistance would have to come from someone else.

The first Easter was certainly a time for many soul-searching questions. We will encounter more of these in the days to come. But for today, let us acknowledge those questions which we ourselves are asking. We all have concerns on our hearts, but they are not always brought out into the open to be resolved. How many of our questions are like those of the women, spoken only in darkness?

These days following Easter, as we pray and reflect, give us the opportunity to face real issues and bring them to the Lord. We may not yet have dared to face some of these problems due to their nature: they remain uncertainties in the dark. And for us, when it comes to these difficult issues, we may find that we empathize with the psalmist who wrote, 'The darkness is my closest friend' (Psalm 88.18).

I find encouragement in the phrase which follows the asking of the women's question in Mark's narrative: 'But when they looked up, they saw that the stone ... had been rolled away.'

'But when they looked up ...' – by lifting their eyes to the place where they believed Jesus was, the women found that God had already provided the answer to their question. He himself had moved the stone.

As we journey towards Ascension Day we will celebrate the return of Jesus to the right hand of the Father. From there he sends his Spirit to work in our lives and bring us to maturity. Offering our concerns to God involves us taking our eyes off the problem and lifting them to him, from whom our help comes. Today let us simply acknowledge our questions, but recognize God's sovereignty over them and place ourselves in his care.

> I lift my eyes to you,
>   to you whose throne is in heaven ...
> Our eyes look to the Lord our God,
>   till he shows us his mercy.
>   (Psalm 123.1–2)

For further reflection

1 Spend some time thinking about questions which you may have and concerns which are on your heart.

- Are you worried or confused about something?
- Do you have doubts about anything?
- Are there issues which you have put off facing, but which periodically resurface?

  Identify as much of the background to these concerns and issues as you can. If it helps, write them down. If an issue has been raised which causes particular concern, you may wish to talk to a trusted friend about this, and ask for their advice and prayers.

2 Try to picture Jesus as our risen Lord. Imagine you are holding your concerns in your hands. Lift you eyes upwards and offer your concerns to him. You may find it helpful to enact this physically. Leave these concerns with him, asking him to show you a way forward. Spend some time in quietness, being open to anything he may want to say to you.

A prayer

Father, I thank you that you are sovereign over all.
There is no issue in my life,
however big or small,
which you cannot handle.
I come to you with my questions.
My love leads me to you despite my concerns.
My questions drive me towards you for answers,
not away from you in puzzlement and dismissal.
I lift my eyes to you
and offer you my very self.
Please show me a way through my difficulties and anxieties.
In Jesus' name. Amen.

Day 3 (Tuesday)

—————— ❦ ——————

A different perspective

'Why do you look for the living among the dead?'
(Luke 24.5)

I well remember the hard work Honor and I had to put
into preparing our first home in time for our wedding day.
I vividly recall late nights decorating what would become
our bedroom. To meet our deadline we had to break
some basic rules of DIY, in particular the one about never
painting by artificial light. We had no choice if we wanted
the room to be ready – so, after full days at work, we
donned old clothes, wielded paint-rollers and burned the
midnight oil. Only in the natural light of the next day did
we see the wisdom of the advice we hadn't followed. Even
a casual glance at the walls and ceiling revealed tell-tale
blotches of unevenness. In the world of decorating, the
light in which you choose to view things makes a big difference to what you see.

The women who came to Jesus' tomb were about to
learn that they were viewing the events of Good Friday in
the wrong kind of light. This is revealed through a searching question from the angel they meet. '"Why do you
look for the living among the dead?"' We have seen that
the women were not expecting Jesus to have risen. So
their natural reaction was to come to the tomb to pay
their last respects. But Jesus was no longer there. God had
already intervened, and the tomb was now empty. The
women were not acting in the light of the resurrection.
Instead, they were living in the light of Jesus' death. Their
perspective was not clear; they had not realized that God
had acted in a way that would make all the difference.

What light are we walking in? Is our perspective on life clear? Has the resurrection really made a difference to us? We may claim to acknowledge the truth of this historical event, and yet aspects of our behaviour may actually be a denial of what God has achieved — like asking forgiveness for a sin which we have already confessed. I have sometimes done this myself, becoming ensnared in guilt through not recognizing the victory of Jesus' resurrection in breaking these chains. Paul challenged the Galatian Christians in regard to this: 'After beginning with the Spirit, are you now trying to attain your goal by human effort?' (Galatians 3.3). The Galatians were no longer living in the light of the resurrection; they were not allowing the power of God, through his Spirit, to be at work in them.

What does living in the light of the resurrection mean to us? Paul, in his classic passage on the resurrection in 1 Corinthians 15, draws five conclusions if the resurrection were untrue:

1. There is no hope of resurrection for anyone who believes in Christ (verse 12).
2. Our faith itself is useless (verses 14, 17).
3. Evangelism is deception as we would be propagating a lie (verse 15).
4. There is no forgiveness of sins (verse 17).
5. Christians are to be pitied more than anyone else (verse 19).

However in verse 20, Paul declares, 'But Christ has indeed been raised from the dead'. Was there ever a more triumphant 'But' uttered in the whole New Testament? It defies all the suppositions which have gone before. Because of the resurrection everything changes:

• Our own resurrection is not a cynical hoax; it's a certain hope.
• Our faith is not futile; it's fruitful.

- Evangelism is not fraudulent; it's fundamental.
- Sin and death are not victorious; they are vanquished.
- We can be proud to bear the name of Christ; we do not need pity.

What's our perspective? The women were shown a different perspective from which to view life. God's intervention had changed everything. How far have these resurrection truths sunk into us? To live with these truths is to live in the full light of Easter. What kind of light are we in? Is it only artificial, or a half-light, or have we fully stepped out of the shadows?

For further reflection

1 Ask the Lord to imprint the truths of the resurrection deep into your heart and life. Work through the five implications of this event mentioned above. Pray that God will further establish the ways in which these truths affect your life. Seek to apply these truths to any situations you are facing at the moment where you sense they can make a difference.

2 You may wish to review one situation you are currently dealing with in the light of today's reading. To help your evaluation, consider the following questions:

- How do I feel about this situation?
- What do I believe God is saying to me through this?
- What am I learning through this, about God, myself and life in general?

3 Pray that you will be open to helping others view their own circumstances in the light of Easter. Be willing to show others how faith in a risen Jesus can make a difference. What would you say to someone who asked your advice about coping with the situation you have highlighted for yourself in the previous exercise?

A prayer

Father, you are the fountain of life;
we see light in your light.
Shine upon me with the light of Easter.
Consume the darkness within me,
and make me a light that shines for you.
For your glory. Amen.

Day 4 (Wednesday)

The God who knows

'I know you are looking for Jesus, who was crucified.'
(Matthew 28.5)

Yesterday we saw how the resurrection changes our perspective on life. The women were challenged to allow God to expand their horizons. This began the process through which their doubts and questions would be resolved. How was it, then, that God came into their confusion to provide a sure foundation of confidence in him? How can this help us with our own doubts and uncertainties? During these next days we will examine several ways in which God intervened.

Today we shall consider God's perfect knowledge of us. The angels at Jesus' tomb said to the women, '"I know you are looking for Jesus, who was crucified."' God, through his angels, declared to them that he knew why they had come. It wasn't a clever, intuitive piece of guesswork; he knew perfectly well. In fact, he was not only declaring that he knew of their motives and actions in the present; he showed them that he was well aware of past events, too – for he spoke of the crucifixion. He himself had watched his Son die, and knew that the women had also witnessed the horror of that day.

God knows our past, present and future: they are all in his sights. He knows the story of our black days – our Good Fridays – just as vividly as the Easter Days. He knows our current situations. He knows the temptations we are facing. He sees the agonizing decisions we are having to make. He is aware of the pressures that threaten to overwhelm us. One of the most common criticisms that

13

can be levelled at us is: 'You just don't understand!' There are also times when we ourselves cry, 'No one understands me!' How often we can be misunderstood. We are judged according to other people's prejudices, labelled under false pretences and neatly filed under categories we ourselves have not even created.

In contrast, with God we encounter the only one who truly understands us. The Old Testament prophets grasped this: 'You understand, O Lord; remember me and care for me' (Jeremiah 15.15); 'The Lord will not tire or grow weary, and his understanding no one can fathom' (Isaiah 40.28).

This is the God to whom we come with our questions, doubts and fears. He is well able to address them; he knows what they are. We can be open with him. He is sympathetic towards us. He does not belittle our questions. He sees them for what they are and knows what lies at their root.

How comforting that he knows! We spend inordinate amounts of emotional energy trying to conceal things from other people – but what a relief that with God we can dispense with pretence. He already knows, and treats us with understanding. And God's perfect knowledge of us is not a distancing intellectualism. He is not like a high-brow professor who lives in an ivory tower, deliberately keeping himself apart from people, believing that his superior knowledge accords him a secure position. No, God draws near to us and seeks to involve himself with us. In response to this, let our questions be a means of drawing us nearer to the Lord, rather than pushing us further from him.

'"Do not be afraid, for I know you are looking for Jesus, who was crucified."' According to Matthew's account, these are the first words spoken to the women following Jesus' resurrection. What was God's first response to the fears of those women? To assure them that he knew why they had come. He understood. This all-knowing God shares his company with us in order that we may share our concerns with him. The 'wonderful counsellor' is near. Trust him with your heart.

For further reflection

1 Psalm 139 is a wonderful celebration of God's perfect knowledge of us. In this psalm, David places his faith firmly in God because of the way in which God understands him. Try to read this passage, and commit yourself to the God who knows. He can be trusted. We can share our concerns with him and invite him to help.

2 God knows about the concerns you offered to him on Day 2. How might his understanding of these help you to face them today?

A prayer

Search me, O God, and know my heart;
test me and know my anxious thoughts.
See if there is any offensive way in me,
and lead me in the way everlasting. Amen.

(From Psalm 139. 23–4)

Day 5 (Thursday)

The God who keeps his word

'Just as he said.'
(Matthew 28.6)

Issues of truth and trust are crucial in life. We rely heavily upon believing what people tell us. We have to trust the advice a doctor gives us when we are ill. We rely on the news we hear to be accurate. We hope our teachers will feed our children correct information.

And these issues of truth are brought more sharply into focus as our society becomes increasingly sceptical of whether anyone is reliable with truth. Innuendo follows innuendo as public figures fall from grace because of ill-judged words; successful prosecutions for libel land the newspapers themselves in the news; 'being economical with the truth' has become an all-too-familiar phrase. In a world such as this, where words seem cheap, who can be trusted? As a friend of mine says, 'We live in a world of truth-decay'.

The women who came to the garden tomb that first Easter morning had not understood Jesus' promise that he would rise again from the dead – so trusting him became an issue for them. Things had looked so promising. Jesus had said so much that was good. But now ... everything had gone so badly wrong. They'd gone from hope to humiliation in a matter of days. Dreams had turned into nightmares – and all because things had apparently not worked out like he said. They had trusted Jesus. He had never let them down before. But now ...

Today we sometimes face issues like this. Circumstances lead us to wonder if God can really be trusted. Reality does not always match up to the promises we believe God to have made – and we are plunged into crisis. If the very source of truth breaks his word, where does that leave us?

Through his angels, God himself came to the rescue of the women, to restore calm to their troubled hearts and minds. And he did this simply by reminding them of what he had said and what he is like. The women had forgotten Jesus' promises that he would rise again. It was time for him to jog their memories. Notice that three of the Gospel writers record their own recollections of the angels' words:

'He is not here; he has risen, just as he said.' (Matthew 28.6)

'… just as he told you.' (Mark 16.7)

'Remember how he told you …' (Luke 24.6)

Do you see what Jesus is getting at? He's saying, in effect, 'Don't you remember what I've told you before? Remember all the times when I promised something – it always came true. And it's no different now. Don't you remember that I said I would rise again?'

What makes you trust someone's words? Isn't it their character which makes the most difference? Character adds credibility to communication. And there's no one who carries finer character references than Jesus.

Cast your own mind back to his life. Remember how the centurion in Capernaum knew that it would only take a word from Jesus to heal his servant: '"But say the word …"' (Luke 7.7). Remember how the royal official took Jesus at his word, to find his dying son restored to life (John 4.50). Remember how the disciples followed Jesus' instructions to prepare the Last Supper and found everything 'just as Jesus had told them' (Luke 22.13).

And it's not just in the New Testament that we find a God who is faithful to his word. How about Abraham and Sarah – an elderly couple, and yet Isaac is born to them, true to God's promise. Solomon, one of the wisest people to have lived, understood God's nature: '"Not one word

17

has failed of all the good promises he gave through his servant Moses"' (1 Kings 8.56). And the psalmist wrote: 'He is faithful to all his promises' (Psalm 145.13).

And God is the same today. He is the God who keeps his word. There is never anything he has promised which he will not fulfil. He is not fickle; his goals are good, and so is his word. His faithfulness is primarily a matter of the integrity of his character. He is Truth with a capital T – and therefore all his actions are derived from this. It is impossible for God to act out of character and be unfaithful to his word: that would be denying his very nature.

Things began to fall into place when the women were reminded of Jesus' promise – 'Then they remembered his words' (Luke 24.8). Just to remember them was enough. For his character authenticated the fulfilment of the promise.

Whom can we trust in these days? In all our uncertainties, one thing stands firm: God's word. It dominates the horizon like a lighthouse shining out over a stormy sea. If you are in the middle of a turbulent storm, look to that lighthouse and remember what God has said. We can trust what he says, simply because he has said it.

When we look back it is always so much easier to see how God has kept his promises. But the real challenge of faith is to take his promises and allow their truth to encourage us forward, even when the future is uncertain. But the faithfulness of God shines out clearly, whichever way we look. He has kept his word down the years, and will continue to do so in all our remaining years.

Yesterday we saw how God began to lay a foundation of confidence in the lives of the women by assuring them that he knew all about them and their concerns. Now he has added a second layer to that foundation: that of his own integrity and faithfulness. You can trust him with *your* words of concern; you can trust him with *his* words of promise. 'God is not a man, that he should lie, nor a son of man, that he should change his mind. Does he speak and then not act? Does he promise and not fulfil?' (Numbers 23.19).

For further reflection

1 Recall times when you feel you have been let down by someone else, because they did not keep their word. Sometimes we can base our own view of God on such experiences, and this makes it hard for us to trust him. Confess to God any occasions that come to mind when you have doubted his promises and his faithfulness to fulfil them. Receive his forgiveness.

2 Ask the Lord to remind you of times in the past when you discovered that he was true to his word. Praise him for his faithfulness. Ask him to sharpen your awareness of future occasions when he proves his word.

A prayer

Father, I praise you for your faithfulness.
All your words can be trusted.
All your promises stand.
Though heaven and earth will pass away,
your words will never do so.
Strengthen my heart with faith in your promises.
For Jesus' sake. Amen.

Day 6 (Friday)

The God who goes ahead

'He has risen from the dead and is going ahead of you.'
(Matthew 28.7)

Today we will be looking at the final layer to the
foundation of confidence which God was building into
the lives of the women, to help them work through the
implications of Easter. He had assured them of his perfect
knowledge of them, and had encouraged them by the
dependability of his promises. If the resurrection really had
changed everything, then others needed to know. How
could the women spread this marvellous news? The
encouragement to get them started is given by the angel
at the tomb: '"He is going ahead of you"'. He is the God
who has gone before.

While on holiday once, my wife and I walked from a
lighthouse, through some coastal woodlands to a remote,
mountainous outcrop. The path was at times completely
obscured, and we had to scramble across bare rock or
through thick undergrowth. Our way, however, was
plotted by small piles of stones, each carefully placed so
that the next pile could always be seen from the previous
one. Thus, guided by these landmarks, we made our way
through the woods to the remote viewpoint.

When returning, however, it became increasingly difficult to see the piles of stones, looking as we were from the
opposite direction. It was almost as if someone had moved
them. Somewhere along the way we must have missed
one – and we got lost, recognizing none of the scenery
around us, and seeing no stones to point the way forward.
There was no alternative but to follow our noses, and so,

praying we'd find the right path, we found ourselves scrambling through dense undergrowth in the failing light. As the darkness closed around us we became increasingly concerned about where to go next, sensing we were a long way from home.

At first our blind adventuring went unrewarded. The light became dimmer, the scenery more obscure, and our adventurous spirits began to give way to concern and fear. Then, bursting suddenly from a tangle of foliage, I looked down to find my feet on a gravel path. And there, just ahead, was a pile of stones pointing the way home. Never have I been so pleased to see a collection of stones! And so, following the path once more, we soon saw the welcoming beam from the lighthouse and duly arrived back at our starting-point – with some scratches and grazes, marks of the adventure we had just been on.

In order for us to walk that path, someone trustworthy had gone before us to place those stones as markers. A previous adventurer had trodden that path, scrambled over those rocks, negotiated the obstacles. We were saved by the careful work of that former traveller. How much more are we saved by the work of our most trustworthy guide and companion, Jesus. Through his life, death and resurrection, Jesus has gone before us in every way, knowing a complete human experience. He is the model for life. Through the life of Jesus, God has blazed a trail, pointing the way. There is nowhere he will ask us to go without having gone before to prepare the way.

When visiting a stately home, we often buy guidebooks to help us. Better still is to have a guide, so that you can ask them further questions. And even better is to be taken round by a friend who is an expert in the place you are visiting. Not only can you ask them all the questions you want, but your relationship ensures that you get personal attention and a tour that picks out the sections in which you would be most interested. But the finest way to see round a stately home is if your friend just happens to be the owner.

Christianity is not primarily a faith to be followed from a guidebook, with no one to turn to for extra help. Christianity is about encountering the author, who is not only with us, but has gone before. His footsteps have trodden the paths. He is aware of pitfalls which may surprise us. He has scaled the mountains and crossed the seas. He has drawn the map. Martin Luther said, 'I do not know the way to go, but well do I know the guide'.

Jesus had gone ahead of the disciples to meet with them and teach the significance of his resurrection. And he is going ahead of us too – into that new job that seems so daunting to us; into that friendship that is proving so difficult; into that community to which you must soon move; into that hospital where you must be treated. 'I'll be there', he says. 'I'll be there when you arrive, and my Spirit will be with you on the journey.'

So take courage when you look ahead. God is already there. For you it may be the great unknown. For him it is familiar territory.

For further reflection

1 What do you see when you look ahead to next week, next month, next year? Is there anything which makes you afraid? Ask God to show you any markers which he has placed to guide you forward. Thank him for any help which he gives. What could you do to be open to his guidance into these situations?

2 Pray for anyone you know who is fearful about a forthcoming event. Ask God to give them a close sense of his companionship at each stage of their journey. Is there anything practical you can do to help them?

A prayer

Lord Jesus
You are the one who goes before
Help me to throw off everything that hinders my
    journey with you.

Protect me from the sins which so easily entangle me.
Help me to run the race with you, fixing my eyes on you alone,
the author and perfector of faith.
I praise you for enduring the cross,
scorning its shame,
and that you are now seated at the right hand of the Father. Amen.

(Based on Hebrews 12.1–2)

Day 7 (Saturday)

When your words seem like nonsense

> But they did not believe the women, because their
> words seemed to them like nonsense.
>
> (Luke 24.11)

God knew very well that when it came to the women
recounting their story, they were going to need all the help
they could get. For the women were told to tell the disciples the best news that could ever be offered to our
broken world, and God knew that the reaction would at
first be very sceptical. If the verse quoted above is anything
to go by, the women's news would have been met with
these kind of responses:

'Nonsense, all nonsense.'

'You're out of your minds. Can't you understand he's
    dead?'

'Telling stories like that won't help any of us come to
    terms with his death.'

Stonewalled with dismissal, rejected with incredulity –
that was the disciples' reaction. To those who have lost
hope, even the very best news can seem like nonsense. The
disciples are trying to get over Jesus' death – but the
women want to tell them that angels have said he is alive!
Maybe it was hard for the women themselves fully to
understand this news. They were, however, able to speak
out of the confidence that God had given them, fleeting
though it may have seemed to them. But at this point, the
disciples had received no such encouragement.

When it comes to speaking good news to people, our
words too can fall on ears which hear but which refuse to

listen. And it is easy to lose heart about ever speaking again. We can judge our words to be feeble and of little importance.

The women could have come up with a long list of reasons why they shouldn't share their news. How many of the following have we caught ourselves thinking when it comes to speaking for God?

- I'm not important enough.
- I don't feel qualified to speak.
- What happens if I'm rejected?
- I'm frightened.
- There are others who are better than me at this.
- I always get muddled with my words.
- I don't have anything to share that could ever make a difference anyway.

Despite concerns such as these, the women chose to speak. Their news was not received well at first. But the actions of the women were finally vindicated as their experiences became those of the disciples. Our words, however feeble they may appear, carry more power than we think. All kinds of things can happen when God breathes life into what we say.

If you have struggled to speak for God, take heart, for you're in good company. Imagine Noah building the Ark. Think of the flak he must have taken as he laboured to complete it – the incredulous comments, the jibes and sneers, the questions about his sanity. Yet he was faithful to God's words and to the warning of the flood to come.

Or take Paul: after his conversion, he went to tell the apostles what God had done for him – and they didn't believe him. They thought he was trying to deceive them and infiltrate their group. It took a brave intervention by Barnabas to accord Paul the credibility he deserved.

Jesus' words were not always well received, either. The Pharisees sneered at him; the Sadducees grumbled; others denounced him; still others picked up stones to kill him. And all because of his words.

Were Noah, Paul or Jesus persuaded not to speak because of their poor reception? Not at all. They understood that God's word is still God's word, however it is received – though we need to be sensitive about how we speak that word.

When it comes to telling of what God has done for us, are we deterred or determined? Let's not become discouraged by our bad experiences. What words could you speak this week which might make a difference? A word of encouragement? Or some advice? Or perhaps you could share your faith with someone?

We may never know the full impact of what we say – our imagined 'failure' must never stop us from speaking out. Unspoken words cannot bless, cannot build up. It is not the quantity – or even the quality – of words which is important; it is our willingness to speak them for God that counts. More than ever we must be people who speak the words of God.

So write that letter – the recipient may treasure it for the rest of their days. Make that phone-call – you could transform a difficult day for someone. Give that encouragement – you never know, you may have given someone just the help they were needing.

God will not waste words we speak for him. The women were the first to share the best news God has ever given humankind. And if we speak too, and join the long line of faithful witnesses, we will have played our part in passing it on.

For further reflection

1 Think about any fears which might be hindering you in speaking about God, or in living fully for him. The suggestions on page 25 may help you to identify some of them.

2 Ask the Lord to heal your memory of any particular incident where your words were not well received, and which has made you fearful to speak again. Ask the

Lord to give you fresh courage. Dwell on the encouragements to speak for God from today's meditation.

3 Is there a letter you could write today, or a phone-call or visit you could make, which could give encouragement to someone? If you think of something, go for it!

A prayer

Lord, you have the words of eternal life.
I praise you for the privilege of speaking for you.
Help me to see that a word spoken for you will never be wasted,
for it carries that same eternal life to bless the one who receives it.
Help me to speak with boldness the words you give me.
May I speak them humbly,
with your authority,
but always in your love.
For Jesus' sake. Amen.

Day 8 (Sunday)

When people made bad news of your good news

They gave the soldiers a large sum of money, telling them, 'You are to say, "His disciples came during the night and stole him away while we were asleep."'

(Matthew 28.13)

In those early days following the resurrection of Jesus, various threats assailed the fledgling faith of the first disciples. Some of these were internal: initial unbelief and astonishment at the resurrection; a lack of understanding of all that had happened; the struggle no longer to rely on Jesus' physical presence. Other threats, however, were external, and Matthew cites one of these. It was the most subtle, yet powerful, attempt to undermine the confidence of Jesus' disciples by making bad news of their good news. It was the power of rumour.

Even before the women had returned with their good news to the other disciples, the tomb-guards had become involved in a plot to discredit them. They claimed that Jesus' body had been stolen by the disciples who were then claiming that he had risen. Bad news was spreading even before the good news had been announced. The result was that all kinds of obstacles and misconceptions had to be overcome.

Have you encountered issues such as these? Battling against the regiments of rumour. They are everywhere, twisting truths and playing endless games of Chinese Whispers down the years to turn authenticity in one generation into speculation in the next. Take, for example what happened during the Falklands War when the

Argentinian military government repeatedly fed false information to their people that they were winning great victories. The depth of the deception was only fully revealed to the Argentinians when the reality of their defeat became known.

What makes rumours so dangerous? First of all, there is a great subtlety about them — the bedrock of truth can soon be covered by dirty spadefuls of small untruths. It doesn't take much to twist a decent truth into a distorted travesty. It only takes one division to make a half-truth from a whole one.

Secondly, rumours get more out of control as they are passed from person to person. In the case of the resurrection, the guards told the chief priests, the chief priests turn to the elders and then the report goes out to the Jews.

Thirdly, rumours can perpetuate untruth down the years. Matthew records that the rumour spread by the guards was still circulating at the time his gospel was written. This was 30 years after the event, yet still the report was being actively propagated. A whole generation had grown up since the resurrection, exposed to a lie. I wonder how many people were taken in by it, never to believe in a risen Jesus. How important it is for us to recognize that we have a responsibility to uphold truth for the next generation to inherit.

For whom do we have responsibility? What truths can we pass on to them? We must remember that it is possible for rumours to be active even among the very people who should most easily dismiss them. The guards' report flourished among the Jews, who should have known the prophecy about the resurrection of the Messiah (Psalm 16.9–10), but did not recognize it, and so were open to other theories.

How do we respond to bad news? Do we crumble? Are we outwitted and outsmarted by a report which places us in a bad light? What happens to us when bad news threatens to sweep our good news away? The disciples would have had to battle against overcoming this opposition to the truth of the resurrection, especially as the guards' report had the added credibility of official support. However, when we look at the story of the Early Church, we do not find reference to this rumour at all. One thing seems clear: it did not discourage the disciples from preaching the resurrection. However strong the rumour was, we find that by the time the Day of Pentecost had come, stronger still was the belief of the disciples that Jesus was alive and that this had to be proclaimed. All kinds of opposition were experienced during the preaching of the gospel in those early days, but preach they did with determination and passion. No amount of rumour was going to stop them. They were heeding the counsel God gave long ago to his people through Jeremiah:

'Do not lose heart or be afraid
    when rumours are heard in the land;
    one rumour comes this year, another the next.'
                (Jeremiah 51.46)

The Apostle Paul was himself a rumour-monger against Christianity, but became a great proclaimer of the truth of the resurrection. After his conversion, he also struggled with opposition from rumours. In 2 Corinthians he describes his determination to pursue his ministry 'through glory and dishonour, bad report and good report' (2 Corinthians 6.8). He knew what it was to have people trying to discredit him, and yet he also knew the God whom he served.

It is easy to be discouraged when rumours abound, even before we have had a chance to state our case. Minds seem to have been poisoned already with an insidious twisting of truth. How do we gain confidence to speak for what's right?

It is God himself who is our confidence. He not only shows us truth; he is Truth. Therefore our confidence to stand up for truth depends not so much on a reliance on abstract facts, but on an authentic person. God is the author of reality – and he has the final say.

We can stand in God's truth by standing in him. Do not be diverted by bad news cutting in on your good news. Do not be discouraged when you set your face against rumours. For Jesus indicated that they would be a constant feature of our society (Matthew 24.6). Instead, let us stand in God's truth and proclaim it boldly. Let reality triumph over rumour!

For further reflection

1 Psalm 112 describes the benefits of trusting the Lord. One of these is outlined in verse 7:

> He will have no fear of bad news;
>   his heart is steadfast, trusting in the Lord.

Read the whole psalm and seek to identify as many ways as you can in which we may learn to trust the Lord more. Pray that you will come to trust him increasingly and so be more firmly rooted in his truth.

2 'See to it that no one takes you captive through hollow and deceptive philosophy, which depends on human tradition and the basic principles of this world … The reality, however is found in Christ' (Colossians 2.8, 17). Think of different opinions, held by people you know, which display a misunderstanding of the Christian faith. Pray that there will be opportunities for you to show the truth of what you believe, particularly in the light of your own personal relationship with the Lord. Pray for your friends to come to a fresh understanding of Christ.

A prayer

Lord of all truth, ground me in the same.
Protect me from attempts to twist that truth into something that is not from you.
Embolden me to stand in your truth and to confront rumour and lies.
Lord of all truth,
I place my trust in you. Amen.

With Mary in the Garden

Mary stood outside the tomb crying. As she wept, she bent over to look into the tomb and saw two angels in white, seated where Jesus' body had been, one at the head and the other at the foot.

They asked her, 'Woman, why are you crying?'

'They have taken my Lord away,' she said, 'and I don't know where they have put him.' At this, she turned round and saw Jesus standing there, but she did not realize that it was Jesus.

'Woman,' he said, 'why are you crying? Who is it you are looking for?'

Thinking he was the gardener, she said, 'Sir, if you have carried him away, tell me where you have put him, and I will get him.'

Jesus said to her, 'Mary.'

She turned towards him and cried out in Aramaic, 'Rabboni!' (which means Teacher).

Jesus said, 'Do not hold on to me, for I have not yet returned to the Father. Go instead to my brothers and tell them, "I am returning to my Father and your Father, to my God and your God."'

Mary of Magdala went to the disciples with the news: 'I have seen the Lord!' And she told them that he had said these things to her.

(John 20.11–18)

Day 9 (Monday)

Grief in the garden

But Mary stood outside the tomb crying.
(John 20.11)

For the next four days we will focus our attention on the episode of Mary Magdalene by the tomb. Her encounter with the risen Christ is deeply moving. We will direct our thoughts in this section towards how Mary's experience can help us when we suffer a time of loss.

I have had the privilege of visiting the Garden Tomb in Jerusalem. Hidden in a bustling district, with a bus station nearby, it is an oasis of peace and tranquillity. From the street, you step through an archway into a most beautiful garden. My reading of this passage of Scripture has always been conditioned by my notion of an English country garden – having now seen a real Middle Eastern garden, the setting of Mary's poignant encounter with Jesus will forever be richer in my imagination. Pathways of loose stones wind their way around beds of tall shrubs. Trees twist their gnarled forms towards the sky; flowers burst from pots in explosions of rich colours. Steps lead to recessed terraces; shady corners compete with areas of full sunlight. In spring, the air is fresh and fragrant with blossom.

No one knows for sure if the Garden Tomb in Jerusalem really was the burial place of Christ. But it certainly gives us an indication of what it must have been like. If we made our way through the real garden, on that first Easter morning, there is one sound which would have been strikingly different from all the others. Come there with me now. Listen – there it is again: the sound of a woman crying. Follow the strains of her weeping – there she is. A young woman stands before a tomb entrance. The stone has been rolled aside; there are grave-clothes lying inside the tomb. The young woman is in great distress. Her face is stained with the tears shed for one she has dearly loved.

Mary Magdalene stands weeping before the empty tomb of her Lord. It is not the first time she has been there. Piecing together the various Gospel accounts, we can deduce that this is her third visit. She was close enough to the tomb when Jesus was buried to know where he was laid (see Mark 15.47, Matthew 27.61). Then came her first visit that Easter morning. On discovering the empty tomb, she runs to Peter and John with her heart's cry on her lips: '"They have taken the Lord out of the tomb and we don't know where they have put him!"'

John 20.1 finds Mary back at the tomb again. She must have returned behind Peter and John, who would probably have outrun her. And now, after the return of Peter and John to their homes, she stands here for the third time. This garden, this simple tomb, is for Mary a place of double grief: she saw her Lord buried here; then she finds the tomb empty and believes his body to be stolen. The resting place of the one she adored has been desecrated. The tomb has been plundered and so has Mary's heart.

Yet Mary has returned, and it is this return that will help her grief turn to joy. But the elation does not come all at once – at first, she fails to recognize the very person she weeps for, because of the depth of her own grief.

There are people, places and incidents in our lives which have been real sources of grief and trouble – perhaps a source of multiple grief, as this was for Mary. Our world is full of them: the friend who betrayed us; the place where a loved one died; the stinging criticism from someone we trusted; the accident which locks up our heart in fear every time we remember it. Memories of these incidents will often come back to us in the years which follow, causing us pain once again.

Mary came back to that place of grief. Perhaps devotion to her Lord brought her to the tomb again. It must have taken a lot of courage for her to revisit that garden. It isn't easy for us either to go back to our own places of grief. But Jesus has a heart to meet us there and begin a work of healing in us. How did this happen for Mary, and how can her story help us in our grief and loss?

Mary sees two angels in white inside the tomb. They ask her '"Why are you crying?"' – another soul-searching question in this post-Easter period. Mary takes an important first step towards her own healing process – she articulates her grief. '"They have taken my Lord away and I don't know where they have put him."'

Pent-up grief is difficult to release. The articulation of our feelings is recognized as a vital ingredient in the process towards working through any sense of loss.

We need not fear sharing our hurt with God. His heart is wide enough to embrace us; his hands are gentle enough to hold a broken heart without causing further damage. Let us take encouragement today to offer him the things which have broken our hearts, along with any sense of loss which we may be experiencing. Often the hurts to which we cling most tightly are the very things he longs to bear for us. The God who opened up the tomb of his Son longs to open up our hearts so that healing life may flow inside.

For further reflection

1 If you are conscious of pain caused by a past event, share your feelings with the Lord. If it helps, talk also with a trusted friend. Beginning to talk about it is an important step in allowing the Lord to heal your pain. Ask the Lord to draw alongside you, as he did with Mary, to give his comfort.

2 Pray for anyone you know who has recently suffered a loss. Ask that the God of all comfort would come close to support them.

3 Ask the Lord to make you more sensitive to the needs
  of others, and to be a good listener.

A prayer

God of all comfort,
I praise you that you are always there to listen.
I offer you the things which have caused me pain,
the losses I have suffered.
In your tenderness, remake my broken heart.
Fill the gaping voids which ache for peace.
And through my own experiences of brokenness
allow me to be a channel of grace to others
who are hurting today.
In Jesus' name. Amen.

Day 10 (Tuesday)

❧

The God who gets our attention

Jesus said to her, 'Mary.'
(John 20.16)

In recent years I have had to attend various clinics at my local hospital. I can remember one of these occasions when, aware of the endless hours of waiting, and to-ing and fro-ing between departments, I armed myself with a good book to pass the time. It was one of the best decisions I had made – as I waited in several different places, I escaped from boredom in the pages of my book. So lost did I become in my reading that only the calling of my name by the nurses was able to attract my attention. And so I journeyed around the hospital, each time lost in my book, yet roused at the sound of my name.

On that first Easter morning, Mary was lost as well – lost in her grief at the death of Jesus. Here is a remarkable thing: Mary looked straight into the eyes of Jesus that morning, but did not recognize him. Her eyes were blurred with tears. The angels and the man before her were just featureless shapes. On the most important morning in the history of the world, Jesus was mistaken for the gardener. The sight of Jesus was not, at that stage, sufficient to pierce the sunless cavern of her grief and disappointment. Something more was needed before the light could penetrate into that dark place.

When Mary failed to recognize Jesus, she felt he'd taken from her what she held most dear: '"Sir, if you have carried him away, tell me where you have put him and I will get him"' (John 20.15). When we grieve after a loss, we can accuse God of robbing us of someone or something that's dear to us. How did Jesus deal with Mary, who was so distraught that she didn't even recognize who he was? How did he help her to recapture her perception of him, and begin a healing work in her heart?

It was his voice that changed everything. One word was all that it took, spoken in a voice that resonated in Mary's heart: 'Mary'. There was no one who spoke her name quite like Jesus did. The sound of her name made life burst within her. 'Rabboni!' she cried. It was Jesus – and this time there was no mistaking him.

Our names are very important – they are the ultimate stamp of our identity. On one occasion my wife, who is a doctor, had to immunize a young boy. She needed to check that she had the correct patient and so asked him his name. 'Michael,' he replied. 'And your surname?' 'I don't know,' he said. 'I don't know that part of my name. I think I was Brown last week, but Mummy has got a new boyfriend now and this week I don't know what I'm called.' That young boy had lost something of his very identity because he did not know his name. God not only knows our name, but calls us by name. The calling of her name not only brought to Mary recognition of Jesus, but began the healing of her grief.

Notice that after Jesus had spoken her name, Mary turned towards him (John 20.16b). This must mean that she wasn't looking at Jesus when he spoke to her. I had always assumed they were face-to-face at that moment. Jesus got Mary's attention even when she was not looking at him. And God seeks to gain our attention, even when our interest is not on him. God will woo us, despite our indifference to him. There was no one who spoke Mary's name quite like Jesus. And there's no one who speaks our own name quite like him.

What an incredible God we have. He does not forget our name. He never has to fumble in his memory-banks to dredge up recognition of who we are. Today let us celebrate the God who is calling us, despite our own desires, which so often distract us from looking to him.

He is a God who will take the initiative and make contact. Our phone may be off the hook but his line is busy trying to get through to us. He is after our attention; he is wanting to speak. You may not be looking at him, but he is still calling. He's calling you by name.

For further reflection

1 Invite the Lord to enter any place of pain you recalled yesterday. Imagine Jesus standing with you and calling your name. What difference does his presence make?

2 Mary had learned to recognize Jesus' voice by listening to him. Pray that your desire to hear him will increase and that you will recognize it more discerningly. What could you do to help you listen more closely to the Lord?

A prayer of praise

It's like you whispered in my ear,
When you saved my soul and brought me near,
That now I am found and I am yours,
And true it's you my heart adores,
I cry out with all that is within,
That I'd never heard a sweeter voice,
Lord you made my aching heart rejoice.
Did angels in your presence sing,
And all the courts of heaven ring,
When you called my name?

(Extract taken from the song "I know your arms are open wide" by Matt Redman. Copyright © 1995 Kingsway's Thankyou Music, PO Box 75, Eastbourne, East Sussex, BN23 6NT, UK. Used by kind permission of Kingsway's Thankyou Music.)

Day 11 (Wednesday)

Known and chosen, protected and valued

Jesus said to her, 'Mary.'
(John 20.16)

Today we will be focusing our attention on some words which God spoke through Isaiah:

'Fear not, for I have redeemed you;
    I have summoned you by name; you are mine.
When you pass through the waters,
    I will be with you;
When you pass through the rivers,
    They will not sweep over you.
When you walk through the fire,
    you will not be burned;
    the flames will not set you ablaze.
For I am the Lord, your God,
    the Holy One of Israel, your Saviour;
You are precious and honoured in my sight
    and ... I love you.
Do not be afraid, for I am with you.'

(Isaiah 43.1–5)

KNOWN

God knows our name because he chooses to have intimacy with us. He does not use our name flippantly. He knows just how special we are. In Luke's Gospel there are only five incidents where Jesus specifically uses someone's name, and they are all at important moments. The way God uses our name is a wonderful sign of his intimacy with us. He knows all about us. He knows the struggles we are having; he feels our grief and sorrows. He understands. Jesus was 'a man of sorrows and familiar with suffering' (Isaiah 53.3). When God speaks our name we hear the tender voice of a father well acquainted with all our ways (Psalm 139.3).

CHOSEN
When God speaks our name we hear the caring voice of one who has chosen us. '"You are mine,"' he declares through the prophet Isaiah. '"I chose you,"' Jesus told his disciples in the upper room during the Last Supper. What a wonderful truth. God singles us out as if we're more important than anyone else. But it's not like at school, where sports captains start choosing team-members in order of their athletic prowess. No, our captain chooses all of us personally.

PROTECTED
The passage from Isaiah 43 about knowing us by name is set within the context of protection: '"Fear not ... do not be afraid, for I am with you"'. When the dark waters of loss threaten to sweep us away, when the raging fire of doubt comes near to consume us – that's when God's presence can comfort us. Have you ever watched the calming effect of a parent holding their frightened child and speaking their name? God is able to hold us better than anyone else can. He speaks our name in reassurance and he sticks by us to see us through.

VALUED
'"You are honoured and precious in my sight and ... I love you."' God has placed enormous value on us. We have been bought at a price. If God even looks after the sparrows, he's bound to think highly of us too (Matthew 6.26). Sometimes we wonder why he even bothers to go on loving us. We often feel we must have let him down just one too many times. But it doesn't affect God's love for us – he may not always approve of what we do, but he always

loves us. For God to know our name, and to call us by name, is a sign of the worth he has invested in us.

I am sure that in some measure, Mary, in that garden, was helped by these things. She must have felt valued and moved that Jesus had met her personally, and her grief disappeared at the realization of his presence.

Known, chosen, protected and valued. That's how God sees us. And this is one way he prepares us for mission. We cannot begin to reach out in his power to serve him until we know we are chosen and valued by him. To communicate how much others are worth to God, we must understand and recognize how much we ourselves are valued. It is often difficult for this truth to sink deep into us. We feel we have let God down too much by our mistakes. But he is more ready to forgive than we are to confess. Let us receive his sense of our worth. This is what happened to Mary, even in the midst of her profound grief. It is an encouragement to know that we too can live in the light of what God thinks of us.

For further reflection

1 Read Isaiah 43.1–5 again, slowly, savouring each phrase. These are God's words to you. Try reading them and inserting your own name to replace 'you'.

2 Choose four people you know, one for each of today's themes; pray that each one will more fully experience that they are either known, chosen, protected or valued by God.

A prayer

Father, I marvel at the way you know me.
You knew me before I was even formed in my mother's womb.
Your eyes have followed all my steps.
Father, I stand in wonder that you have chosen me.
You call me your friend, and seek intimacy with me.
You have never given up on me.

Father, I am so in need of your protection.
The world is dark and dangerous; the enemy is at work.
I need you to be my fortress.
Father, how can it be that you value me as your very own?
I feel so worthless sometimes, and have hurt you so often.
And yet the price you paid for us is the true value you
   choose to place on us:
the price of your own Son.
Father, I am so grateful to be yours. Amen.

Day 12 (Thursday)

Moving on

Mary of Magdala went to the disciples with the news:
'I have seen the Lord!'

(John 20.18)

Following her recognition of Jesus, Mary took two further
important steps to move on from her encounter with him.
These can be helpful for us in cultivating an ongoing
awareness of God's presence.

First of all she had to learn not to cling to Jesus' physical presence. Mary must have been so ecstatic to see Jesus
that she went to embrace him, because Jesus tells her: '"Do
not hold on to me, for I have not yet returned to the
Father"'.

Mary had just learned that the grave could not hold
Jesus. She still had to learn that she could not hold him
either. Jesus knew the importance of not letting Mary
cling to his physical presence. He knew that he was
ascending to the Father, and he had already told his disciples that it would be better for them if he did. He could
then send the Holy Spirit, through whom they could
enjoy his presence wherever they were. Mary had to learn
to release the immediate physical presence of Jesus in
order to receive the gift of his presence through his Holy
Spirit.

It is an important step for us, as we move on from a
healing encounter with Jesus, that we do not cling to that
moment, but go on trusting in the Lord and allowing him
space to work in us. Such meetings with Jesus are milestones for us, and it is good to remember what he did for
us at those times. But we must not try and stay at the mile-

stone, without moving on – otherwise the milestone will only become a millstone. We can so easily live in the past, and not take up our personal responsibility to press on to maturity in Christ. An awareness of God in our present-day lives cannot be strengthened when we focus too much on past experiences.

Secondly Mary gave testimony. Jesus told her, '"Go … to my brothers and tell them"'. Mary went with her news to the disciples. '"I have seen the Lord!"' was her delighted cry. What a contrast to the last words she spoke to them. Then she'd been frightened and confused – now she has great joy.

She was able to testify to what Jesus had done for her. This can be another helpful step in moving on with him. Speaking of what he has done brings home the reality of his work in us, and earths in us a confidence in what he has done. Telling others about our encounters with Jesus can bring to us a greater appreciation of him, and cultivate in us a deeper perception of what he will do in the future. Secure because we know he loves us and knows us by name, we can go and tell others about what he has done for us.

If you are living in the cavern of despair and grief, remember the story of Mary. Take courage in your heart, and revisit the place of grief. You will find that Jesus is wanting to meet you there too. The psalmist wrote:

> But you, O God, do see trouble and grief;
> you consider it to take it in hand.
> (Psalm 10.14)

Our Father is watching over us. He is not unaware of our sorrow. Mary at first missed who Jesus was, but that doesn't have to be the case for us. Grief and loss don't have to hold us forever. Mary's tale shows us that when Jesus speaks, it can make all the difference. He calls us by name. We are his; known, valued, chosen and protected. His words can change everything. And who knows? For us, like Mary, it may only take one word. And this time, the name on his lips will be ours.

For further reflection

1 What events do you perceive as being important milestones in your journey of faith? Thank God for what he was doing in your life at that time. How have you moved on from these times?

2 Aim to share one of these important milestone experiences with someone else in the coming week. Ask the Lord to guide you to the person he wants you to share with, and to give you the right words.

A prayer

Lead me, Lord, take me on.

Help me to see the landmarks that chart my progress with you.

Never let me forget how far you have brought me,

for there are many who would seek to discourage me from continuing the journey.

And every time I get stuck, help me to see a landmark that speaks of how you've led me on,

and causes faith to rise within me that you can take me further still.

For Jesus' sake. Amen.

On a Journey to Emmaus

Now that same day two of them were going to a village called Emmaus, about seven miles from Jerusalem. They were talking with each other about everything that had happened. As they talked and discussed these things with each other, Jesus himself came up and walked along with them; but they were kept from recognizing him.

He asked them, 'What are you discussing together as you walk along?'

They stood still, their faces downcast. One of them, named Cleopas, asked him, 'Are you only a visitor to Jerusalem and do not know the things that have happened there in these days?'

'What things?' he asked.

'About Jesus of Nazareth,' they replied. 'He was a prophet, powerful in word and deed before God and all the people. The chief priests and our rulers handed him over to be sentenced to death, and they crucified him; but we had hoped that he was the one who was going to redeem Israel. And what is more, it is the third day since all this took place. In addition, some of our women amazed us. They went to the tomb early this morning but didn't find his body. They came and told us that they had seen a vision of angels, who said he was alive. Then some of our companions went to the tomb and found it just as the women had said, but him they did not see.'

He said to them, 'How foolish you are, and how slow of heart to believe all that the prophets have spoken! Did not the Christ have to suffer these things and then enter his glory?' And beginning with Moses and all the Prophets, he explained to them what was said in all the Scriptures concerning himself.

As they approached the village to which they were going, Jesus acted as if he were going further. But they urged him strongly, 'Stay with us, for it is nearly evening; the day is almost over.' So he went in to stay with them.

When he was at the table with them, he took bread, gave thanks, broke it and began to give it to them. Then their eyes were opened and they recognized him, and he disappeared from their sight. They asked each other, 'Were not our hearts burning within us while he talked with us on the road and opened the Scriptures to us?'

(Luke 24.13–32)

Day 13 (Friday)

Disappointment road

'But we had hoped …'
(Luke 24.21)

It's only about seven miles from Jerusalem to Emmaus – not a long walk really. But any walk is hard when you have a heavy load on your back. And it's harder still when you have a heavy heart. That was the case for Cleopas and his friend. You can see them now on the road: their postures tell it all – feet dragging, shoulders hunched, faces down-cast. They're not just walking the Emmaus road. They're also trudging the road of disappointment.

Many in the Bible can testify to this. Take Job for example: '"My days have passed, my plans are shattered and so are the desires of my heart"' (Job 17.11). The writer of Proverbs knew the same truth: 'Hope unfulfilled makes the heart sick' (Proverbs 13.12).

That's Cleopas and friend in a nutshell: sick of heart from dashed hopes. They've been witnesses of the last days of Jesus' life: betrayal and beatings, brutality and burial. In their minds, Jesus is dead – and their hope died with him. Confusion and disappointment cloud their minds – their conversation is dominated by the loss of their master.

And as they walk on, the most amazing adventure unfolds. Jesus himself draws alongside and joins the two disciples, but they don't recognize him. That's what can happen when disappointment and discouragement – the Devil's favourite weapons – dominate our thoughts and sadden our hearts. There is an old legend about God deciding to reduce the weapons in the Devil's armoury to one. Satan, allowed to choose which fiery dart he would

49

keep, chose the power of discouragement. 'If only I can persuade Christians to be thoroughly discouraged,' he reasoned, 'they'll make no further effort.' That's the point at which we find Cleopas and his companion.

We can often be on the same road. In this situation we can miss the very presence of God beside us. He is near, but hidden by a thick veil of unfulfilled expectations covering us. He'll be a stranger on the road. Even if our heart is burning within us, that's no guarantee we'll notice him. Cleopas and his friend certainly didn't.

They clearly aren't a happy pair. Their downcast faces tell the whole story. Maybe you feel you've walked that long road of disappointment for too long now. Perhaps your disappointment may even be with God himself, because you feel he has not acted as you thought he would. When you think about certain things in your life, you can so easily echo Cleopas' words: 'But we had hoped …'. The rug of their own expectations had been pulled from under them. They had lost the foundation of their faith, and were struggling to make sense of current events. If this is you, you've probably talked it all through; just like Cleopas and his friend. But you're still left disillusioned and seeking some answers.

The encouragement of this story is that Jesus came alongside. The road you are on is not too isolated for Jesus to find. He has the whole map before him. The terrain might look bleak, but it's not uncharted territory for him. He is wanting to meet us at our place of disappointment. You can keep him distant if you like, but he is longing to come alongside to draw from us our own feelings of frustration and to minister to our hurts.

For further reflection

1 Bring to the Lord any recent disappointment you have suffered. Share your feelings with him, just as Cleopas and his friend talked to Jesus on the Emmaus road.

2 Ask the Lord to come alongside you and to take you on from your place of disappointment.

A prayer

Lord of all hope,
meet me on my road of disappointment.
Walk with me as you did that Emmaus road so long ago.
Let me hear your footsteps beside me.
Thank you that you know just how long I've walked down
    this road,
and that you desire to be a comforting companion. Amen.

Day 14 (Saturday)

False expectations

'We had hoped that he was the one who was going to redeem Israel.'

(Luke 24.21)

Yesterday we saw how disappointment can cloud the way we see God and relate to him. The story of events on the Emmaus road reveals factors which contributed to the disappointment experienced by Cleopas and his friend.

First of all their expectations were false. The two travellers misunderstood Jesus' mission. They lament over Jesus' arrest and execution and add, 'But we had hoped that he was the one who was going to redeem Israel'. They obviously thought that the Passion was a big mistake. The crucifixion of Jesus was not their idea of God playing his winning hand. 'What a waste!' they were probably thinking. Perhaps they had in mind Jesus as a triumphant king, rescuing the Jewish nation from the tyranny of the Romans. Whatever they were thinking, the events in Jerusalem had brought them real disillusionment.

False expectations can't help us when we're walking on the road of disappointment. Often they are the signposts that lead us on to that road in the first place. As long as Cleopas and his friend believed what they did about Jesus, they were going to walk that long road of disappointment. Why did they make wrong assumptions about Jesus?

The story shows that they didn't understand the Scriptures. '"How foolish you are, and how slow of heart to believe all that the prophets have spoken!"' That's quite a rebuke from Jesus. The Greek word used here for 'foolish' literally means 'mindless ones'. The two travellers didn't know God's plan from the Scriptures. If they had known, they would have understood the place of the Messiah's death. They would have rejoiced over its purpose and would have been looking forward to the resurrection. What should have been a spring of joy was a source of sorrow.

We can react to life in a very topsy-turvy manner when we misunderstand God's purposes in Scripture. There is a rich seam of revelation waiting to be mined. Possessing a firm biblical perspective is vital for balance in our thoughts and actions. Without this, our perspective, like that of the travellers on the Emmaus road, is distorted, as if we are viewing life through a cracked window. Could this be true of us?

False expectations invariably lead us to adopt mistaken opinions about God. This was certainly true in this story. Cleopas thought Jesus didn't understand: '"Are you only a visitor to Jerusalem and do not know the things that have happened?"' Blinded by his distorted perspective, Cleopas asks this ironic question of the very person who was at the centre of the drama. The person whose knowledge of the situation is challenged is the very person who will bring Cleopas and his friend to a full comprehension of all that has happened.

How did Jesus help these two bewildered disciples? He explained the Scriptures to them: 'And beginning with Moses and all the prophets, he explained to them what was said in all the Scriptures concerning himself.' Cleopas and his companion are a privileged pair. It's not every day you get treated to a Bible study led by Jesus himself. They got the full works: 'He explained … *all* the Scriptures concerning himself.'

False expectations need changing. Moving off the road of disappointment comes by knowing the heart, mind and purposes of God. 'For everything in the past was written to teach us, so that through endurance and the encouragement of the Scriptures, we might have hope' (Romans 15.4).

Hope can be restored by the truth of Scripture. This is what Jesus was doing on the Emmaus road. He took

Scripture and let its power rekindle hope within his two fellow-travellers. Perhaps this is what we ourselves need. Have we forgotten to let the Bible encourage us? Has it just stayed on the shelf recently, weighing it down, when we ourselves have been weighed down with discouragement? Or do we read it with a sense of drudging routine, hardly believing that it carries God's power to make a difference? Scripture *is* powerful, but only if we let it into our lives. As I read recently on a poster: 'If our Bible is falling apart, then we won't be'.

'A longing fulfilled is a tree of life' (Proverbs 13.12) – and Jesus is about to make that tree surge with fresh life for Cleopas and his friend. He had prepared the ground by restoring their view of God's purposes in Scripture. Their own expectations of Jesus are changed, even though they haven't yet recognized him. Now a choice is laid before them.

'As they approached the village … Jesus acted as if he were going further.' Here is a little bit of drama by the world's centre-stage character: Jesus makes as if he's going further. Why? Perhaps he was seeing how well he'd got through to his two fellow travellers. They had a choice: they could let Jesus go, or they could continue their voyage of discovery. God doesn't force himself on us. There are times when we can let him go, rather than spend time with him. But he always responds to our invitation to come and stay. So let us welcome him into our homes and life's concerns.

For further reflection

1 Ask God to increase your desire to read his word in the Bible. As you read, allow God to transform any wrong assumptions you may have made about him.

2 Why not commit yourself to memorize at least one new Bible verse each week? This is a great way to allow God's word to penetrate our lives.

A prayer

Lord, forgive me for the times when I have acted out of a misunderstanding of you.

More than ever, deepen my relationship with you.

I want to know you, Lord.

Help me to encounter you in a deeper way through Scripture.

May your Spirit bring your word more alive to me.

I want to enter more fully into a relationship of intimacy and trust.

Draw me closer, Lord. Amen.

Day 15 (Sunday)

Mementoes

When he was at the table with them, he took bread,
gave thanks, broke it and began to give it to them. Then
their eyes were opened and they recognized him, and
he disappeared from their sight.

(Luke 24.30–31)

What was it that made the difference? Did Cleopas and his
friend see the scars on Jesus' hands? Was it his thanksgiving prayer? Was it the way Jesus broke the bread? All we
know is that as the bread was broken, so the veil was lifted
from their eyes. It was then that they recognized him.

Breaking bread was a familiar action. Perhaps the two
travellers had witnessed the way Jesus had fed the multi-
tudes, or broken bread in someone's home. God helps us
to recognize him in familiar things. He'll show us the verse
that's meant so much to us. We'll see him in that friend we
love so dearly. God doesn't waste our past: he can use it to
build our future. He places milestones in our lives for a
purpose – they're like landmarks. Whether we realize it or
not, he's leaving behind mementoes of his presence that
will remind us of him.

Jesus disappeared from the two disciples as soon as they
recognized him. Only the broken bread and their burning
hearts told them he'd been there. Yet that was enough,
because broken bread had replaced broken dreams, and
burning hearts had replaced sorrowful lives. Simple
mementoes of a close encounter with the Son of God.

Let's be aware of the souvenirs God is leaving in our
lives. They may seem insignificant today, but in several
years' time the memory of them could make the difference

between catching a fresh glimpse of God, or missing him and trudging on a road that seems to go nowhere.

Are you good at keeping mementoes? When we got married, and Honor and I merged our belongings, we saw an interesting difference between us. Before marriage, I tended not to have knick-knacks around my house; Honor, by contrast, had a host of fascinating items collected from different places and people, all of them with a good story to explain their origin. I now see how helpful such mementoes can be, and since knowing Honor I've enjoyed having some very visual reminders of good times we've had and people we've met.

We have our mementoes displayed – but we've seen that other people can hide theirs away and not appreciate them. Honor and I stayed at a bed and breakfast establishment recently and noticed a beautiful set of what we learned was wedding crockery, sitting in crumpled plastic bags gathering dust in a Welsh dresser. They must have sat there for years – a poignant reminder of a very special occasion, yet never enjoyed or valued.

What do we do with the mementoes which God is leaving with us? Those memories of special times when we have met with him, for example? Do we cherish them, or package them up and file them away out of sight so that we never really see them? If you have boxed some away, why not re-discover them and dust them down? Give them a good polish and reflect on the truth behind them. You might be surprised by the gracious way in which God has treated you. After all, he treats you as someone very special. You are a trophy of his grace. Isn't it time we gave our special memories of him a better place?

For further reflection

1   Think back to the important milestones you brought to mind on Day 12. Remembering what you learned through those experiences, is there anything which you could helpfully apply to an issue which concerns you today?

2 Try starting a journal in which you record special
   memories of your journey with the Lord. It will
   provide a rich source of encouragement for you in
   future years. What could you write down today?

A prayer

Lord, I thank you for the mementoes you have left behind
   for me.
They are souvenirs of grace, treasures of your love.
And of all that you have given,
I praise you most of all
for the costliest symbol of love – your cross. Amen.

Day 16 (Monday)

Out of our comfort zone

They got up and returned at once to Jerusalem.
(Luke 24.33)

I recently heard two church leaders telling about a frightening experience they'd had on a plane recently. The pilot announced on the intercom that the plane had developed problems. He had to turn the plane around and head back to Heathrow airport, from where they had taken off only two hours earlier. On the return journey it was necessary to jettison most of the fuel, and preparations were made at Heathrow for an emergency landing.

On approaching the runway, the pilot announced that he did not have full control of the air-flaps on the plane, and so all the passengers were asked to assume the emergency crash position (leaning forward in their seats with their heads buried in their arms).

The landing was extremely rough, and it took a long time to bring the plane finally to rest. The emergency services were all waiting at the end of the runway, but they weren't needed. No one had been injured; but it had clearly been an incident which had shaken all those on board. You could certainly say that all those passengers had been taken outside their own comfort zones.

Scary, isn't it, to be thrust beyond the things with which we feel safe and with which we are familiar? Life can already feel like walking on a tightrope, but when someone folds away the safety net, the ground looks an awful lot further away.

Cleopas and his friend were about to realize how the impact of meeting Jesus would take them out of their own comfort zone. The true reality of the risen Christ had just dawned on them. The pair then had a choice. There they sat at the meal-table; they were still holding the bread Jesus had given them. But they were holding something more precious still: the truth of the resurrection. What would they do? It would have been so comfortable just to stay where they were. After all, they hadn't even finished their meal, the house was cosy, and they could have contentedly sat chatting for hours, resting their weary feet from walking seven miles.

I remember staying away from home on a wild night, when the wind howled round the building, making the autumn leaves dance and chase one another in the air. How snug I felt in my bed. I curled deeper beneath the covers. It would have been hard to entice me from such a comfortable cocoon.

We are sometimes more interested in our own comfort than in moving out to do God's work. We prefer our present status; our surroundings suit us; there are necessary tasks to complete.

What about Cleopas and his friend? For them there was no dilemma – they had to tell the apostles the news. It was time to leave their comfortable surroundings and go out into the night. For night it was (remember that the evening was already near when they had arrived in Emmaus). By the time Jesus broke bread it would have been dark – but into the night they went. It was no mean feat to retrace those seven miles at night. That's a long way to go when you can't see very far in front of you. But the passion of their encounter with Jesus spurred them on.

How do we feel about moving out in this way? The world is still full of darkness. And to declare ourselves available to God, to bring his good news into that darkness, is to take ourselves out of our comfort zones. The start of being commissioned by God is to recognize the darkness of our world and to prepare to be light there. Cleopas and his companion had already been commissioned on the road to Emmaus, when, with burning hearts, they had received God's word. And with those hearts still on fire they took the light of Easter back through the darkness.

The novelist Robert Louis Stevenson once watched an old lamp-lighter move down his road, lighting the street lamps. 'Do you enjoy your work?' Stevenson asked. 'It's a fine thing to punch holes in the darkness,' came the reply. What can we do to punch holes in the darkness we see around us?

For further reflection

1 What are the boundaries of your own comfort zone? Identify any recent experiences which have pushed back these boundaries. How did you feel at the time? How was it that you were able to leave your comfort zone?

2 The prophet Jeremiah know what it was for God's word to burn in his heart:

> But if I say, 'I will not mention him
>   or speak any more in his name,'
> his word is in my heart like a fire,
>   a fire shut up in my bones.
> I am weary of holding it in;
>   indeed I cannot.
>
> (Jeremiah 20.9)

Pray that God's word would so burn in your heart that you would be prepared to go the extra mile in sharing the good news with others.

3 Pray that the Lord would open up more opportunities for you to speak for him.

A prayer

Lord, I do not know the future,
so I place my hand in yours.
The winds of change may blow me on a different course,
out of my comfort zone.
Yet you are always with me;
I seek my safety in you.
Help me to step out in faith
knowing that as I do, your hand still holds me tight.
For your glory, I pray. Amen.

Day 17 (Tuesday)

Time to dream again

'Were not our hearts burning within us while he talked
with us on the road and opened the Scriptures to us?'

(Luke 24.32)

Today we conclude our journey with Cleopas and his
friend. Graham Kendrick has retold their story in a song
called *Comforting Stranger*. The words are worth quoting in
full. Read the words slowly. Respond to them, savouring
the story we have examined over these days.

I took my walking shoes and made for the road,
And as we were leaving the air turned cold.
Just the starlight and you and a stone in my shoe
And then suddenly there was this stranger,
The Comforting Stranger is still on the road.
We told him our sorrows, the loss of a friend,
The cross and the traitor, the bitter end.

He walks me down my life-long street and fills my empty
    spoon,
Beside the greenest fields he lays me down.
He leads me by still waters and revives my hungry soul.
If you see his lamp approaching you will know he's still
    on the road.

Bread on the table, the wood on the fire,
Three firelight shadows flickering higher.
The wine in the firelight turned richer red.
'This wine is my blood,' he said, 'my body this bread.'

Like a voice that is caught by the wind, he was gone,
And then suddenly I knew the Stranger,
The Comforting Stranger is still on the road.

The Emmaus road story teaches us about a God who, like a comforting stranger, comes alongside to restore hope and to teach us to dream.

In our past we may be able to identify dreams which we longed for God to fulfil. At those times we were sure they were part of God's will for us. And we prayed earnestly for him to bring them to pass in our lives. But nothing seemed to happen. And we waited and prayed … but still nothing. And so we stopped hoping, just like Cleopas and his friend. But the reason we ceased to pray was not because God had told us that it wasn't his will – we simply tired of waiting. It was too much to keep hoping and praying for something that never seemed to come. No guilt should be attached to us for this – it's very understandable when we can't keep going.

The Emmaus road story encourages us to pick up some of those dreams again, those long-cherished hopes which we have dared not entertain – possibly for many years. God is saying it is time to dream again, time to pray again, for those things. We were never wrong to believe them originally; it is just that God's timing for us is very different from what we first imagined. But the time is now coming soon when he wants to bring these things about. He encourages us to pray again to co-operate with him in what he is doing.

Does something stir in you when you read that? Do you sense that God is prompting you to recognize that this could relate to you? If so, begin to dream those dreams again. Perhaps share this with some friends, and ask them to pray with you about this.

All of us need the encouragement of God in our walk with him. There are, however, occasions when we need this more than usual – and times of disenchantment are prime examples. The road of disappointment can easily entice the unwary and weary traveller. That road is a hard one to navigate. If you're walking that road today, remember Jesus can meet you. His words and presence can bring encouragement and make that tree of life blossom within us.

He says, 'Those who hope in me will not be disappointed' (Isaiah 49.23). So next time you have your eyes on your broken dreams, just glance to your left and your right, as you can never be sure who you might have travelling with you. And next time you are gazing back at all your bridges burning, just take a peek inside at your own heart, because if that is burning too, then the comforting stranger may be closer than you think.

For further reflection

1 Lay before the Lord any long-cherished dreams which have never been fulfilled. Ask him to show you if this is the time for you to dream them again. Be open to co-operating with the Lord on this.

2 Review what you have learned from journeying on the Emmaus road.

A prayer

Lord, teach me to dream dreams of your making,
stir visions of faith within me.
Not vain hopes of my own persuasion,
but passionate goals full of your intention.
God of all hope,
Teach me to dream again. Amen.

Day 18 (Wednesday)

Postscript to Emmaus:
an untold story

'The Lord has risen and has appeared to Simon.'
(Luke 24.34)

There are many untold stories surrounding that first Easter
Day. If we could enter the minds of each of the characters,
we would discover an amazing array of emotions and
complex thoughts. Recounting them all would yield a
Gospel for every one of the disciples. There is one untold
event, however, which deserves mention. It is at the end of
the Emmaus story that we first learn of a further appearance
by Jesus which had already taken place by the time Cleopas
and his friend arrived in Jerusalem. The travellers from
Emmaus find the other disciples declaring, '"It is true! The
Lord has risen and has appeared to Simon"' (Luke 24.34) –
an incident also mentioned by Paul in 1 Corinthians 15.5.
Bearing in mind the chronology of that first Easter Day,
these references indicate that Jesus met Simon Peter sometime between mid-morning and the afternoon.

For Peter, the first part of that day had been so eventful.
It had been very black for him since Friday, ever since that
time in the courtyard of the high priest. He may have felt
worse than all the other disciples, because he was the one
who had denied Jesus with his lips – the same lips which
earlier had sworn allegiance unto death. For the last two
days he was probably haunted by the face of Jesus looking
at him from across the courtyard as the cock crowed. It
was the last time he had seen Jesus alive.

And then strange events began to unfold that Sunday.
Early on, Peter was surprised by the women's news: the

empty tomb, angels, grave-cloths – but no Jesus. Peter and John ran to investigate. Peter entered the tomb and saw the linen burial cloths and the separated head-cloth. There was something very unusual about those cloths. It was just as if the body had vanished from within them and the material had collapsed under the weight of the spices. Something was up.

All we know from Scripture is that sometime within about half a day of the discovery of the empty tomb, Peter encounters its former occupant – now very much alive. What took place in those moments is not recorded for us. Those of us who now look back at such things across the centuries can only stand and wonder at the grace and tenderness of the risen Christ who chose quite deliberately to meet with Peter, just for him.

We do not know what words were spoken between them. Perhaps it was not a time for words anyway. The fact that Jesus was there for Peter was the most important thing. I expect there was much emotion: tears, perhaps of relief, joy and contrition on Peter's part. This was more a time of reassurance for Peter than anything else. He had already shown his remorse for his denial. His tears of shame and anger at his actions must have been shed often over those days. What no one had been able to give him was comfort, to show him that there was a way out for him. Maybe in his blackest moments he felt himself falling helplessly towards the fate of Judas. The other disciples may not have realized the depth of his sorrow. 'Don't you see that nothing matters any more to me, not now that he's gone, and after what I've done,' he might have said. He was repentant, but unforgiven; sorrowful, yet comfortless. There was no one to ease his pain; no one to give a fresh start – until Jesus came back for him.

This poignant meeting began the healing process within Peter for his failures on Good Friday. It is clear that this process wasn't completed until the encounter between them by the Sea of Galilee (as we will see on Day 31). Peter must have needed time for his emotions to catch up with his will, for it is the latter which Jesus addressed in that subsequent encounter.

This first encounter was to bring hope to Peter, who felt that he had failed once too often, that he had gone too far over the edge. Jesus showed Peter that he had come back, not just for the other disciples, but for him as well. This encounter brings hope to all those who have lost faith that God will bring a blessing to them. We see others experience a close walk with the Lord, or we witness a particular blessing they receive – but we reason that such things are not for us. We don't think that God will meet *us* in a special way. We collect all kinds of reasons why God should choose to avoid us: unworthiness, not good enough, too young, too old. But God is not distanced by such things. He just wants us to desire fellowship with him. Even Peter's denials could not keep Jesus from coming back for him. Because deep down, it was Peter's desire to have Jesus back again too.

Peter was the first of the remaining eleven disciples to see the risen Christ. If Jesus had shown himself first to all the disciples at once, I can imagine Peter feeling that Jesus had come back just for them, but not for him. 'I just happen to be here,' he might have said, 'but I'm not the reason he's come – he wouldn't do it just for me.' Jesus demonstrated through this personal encounter that that is exactly why he had come back – he had conquered the grave for everyone, including Peter. And he has done it for each one of us also. Jesus' action highlighted beyond any doubt that Peter was not forgotten. And he has not forgotten us either – he has come for us too.

For further reflection

1 Examine your own heart for any attitude which makes you feel that God has forgotten you in some way, or will not bring his blessing to you. How could Jesus' special encounter with Peter help you address this issue?

2 Think back to the concerns you brought to mind on Day 2. As you have journeyed with the disciples beyond Easter for these last two weeks, how do these issues now seem? Pray again about them in the light of what the Lord has been saying to you.

A prayer

Lord, how can it be that you don't forget me?
You call me to mind,
you're never unaware of my ways.
I could never understand this
and so I just marvel.
Help me to marvel more
and never to forget
that with you I am never forgotten. Amen.

In the Upper Room

On the evening of that first day of the week, when the disciples were together, with the doors locked for fear of the Jews, Jesus came and stood among them and said, 'Peace be with you!' After he said this, he showed them his hands and his side. The disciples were overjoyed when they saw the Lord.

Again Jesus said, 'Peace be with you! As the Father has sent me, I am sending you.' And with that he breathed on them and said, 'Receive the Holy Spirit. If you forgive anyone his sins, they are forgiven; if you do not forgive them, they are not forgiven.'

(John 20.19–23)

They were startled and frightened, thinking they saw a ghost. He said to them, 'Why are you troubled, and why do doubts rise in your minds? Look at my hands and my feet. It is I myself! Touch me and see; a ghost does not have flesh and bones, as you see I have.'

And while they still did not believe it because of joy and amazement, he asked them, 'Do you have anything here to eat?' They gave him a piece of broiled fish, and he took it and ate it in their presence.

He said to them, 'This is what I told you while I was still with you: Everything must be fulfilled that is written about me in the Law of Moses, the Prophets and the Psalms.'

Then he opened their minds so they could understand the Scriptures. He told them, 'This is what is written: The Christ will suffer and rise from the dead on the third day, and repentance and forgiveness of sins will be preached in his name to all nations, beginning at Jerusalem. You are witnesses of these things. I am going to send you what my Father has promised; but stay in the city until you have been clothed with power from on high.'

(Luke 24.37–9, 41–9)

Day 19 (Thursday)

Ready for action?

'As the Father has sent me, I am sending you.'
(John 20.21)

The appearance of Jesus to this group on the evening of that first Easter Day represented a distinct shift in the way he was dealing with them. Up till now, he had been seeking to address specific doubts and questions with which the disciples were struggling. Although some of these issues still persisted, the language of Jesus revealed that he had a mission in mind.

"'As the Father has sent me, I am sending you.'" (John 20.21)

"'You will be my witnesses.'" (Luke 24.48)

"'Go and make disciples.'" (Matthew 28.19)

Jesus was preparing to send out his followers to be bearers of the good news of his resurrection. After confronting some of the disciples' questions and doubts, how did Jesus begin the first stage of sending them out?

Notice the words he chose to speak. The first words of the risen Jesus heard by some of those disciples were, "'Peace be with you'". He came through locked doors to speak that peace. They could not keep him out – the walls were not impenetrable for him. And the walls that we put up today – walls of fear, doubt, unacceptableness, inexperience, age – these are not impassable for the peace and presence of Christ. He comes to grant us this peace to guard our hearts and minds (Philippians 4.7). This is important preparation for serving the Lord. Our hearts and minds need to be surrounded by the peace of Christ and our lives need to be full of his Spirit.

Jesus then showed the disciples the wounds of his Passion. Before we can be sent out to do God's work we need to see afresh the extent of Christ's love for us. Some of the disciples had not seen him die, and they now saw for themselves the physical signs of his sacrifice for them. Even those who had seen him die probably didn't fully realize that he was doing it for them. They considered it to be a ghastly and terrible mistake. As Jesus showed them his hands, feet and side, maybe his words at the Last Supper began to ring in their ears: '"Greater love has no one than this, that he lay down his life for his friends"' (John 15.13).

Suddenly all the purpose and the meaning of his suffering became clear. And the most remarkable thing was that at the heart of the purpose of the cross was a love for each one of the disciples. And for us.

We can only speak of God's love to the extent that we know it ourselves. It is hard to convey that Jesus died for someone else if we have not accepted that he gave his life for us also.

Jesus was showing his disciples just how much he had given for them. It became a powerful motivation for them in spreading the good news. Paul wrote, 'Christ's love compels us' (2 Corinthians 5.14). The Greek word he used for 'compels' actually means 'to constrain, to hold together' – it conveys the idea of being captivated. A well-known firm of car manufacturers had the slogan: 'Once driven, forever smitten'. This is something of the concept which Paul was trying to explain. He was saying that we've been love-struck by God to such an extent that it affects the very way we think, speak and live.

No wonder the disciples were overjoyed. They were seeing not just the return of their master, but were experiencing the full recognition of all that he had given for them. His wounds spoke louder than any words he himself could say. Those wounds declared, 'I did it for you'.

Jesus came to commission a group of characters whom the world would have dismissed as being wholly unfit for the task assigned to them:

- They were not all together that first evening – Thomas was not there.
- They were still scared of the Jews, despite the news of his resurrection that was filtering through.
- They had deserted their master in his hour of need.

They did not seem a likely group to succeed. But it is not the world who is making the choice here: it is Jesus. He was the one calling the tune. Perhaps you have already signed yourself off the list of those whom Jesus might choose to make a difference in the world for him. Maybe you consider yourself unfit for duty.

The most important thing about Jesus' choice was that the qualification for service was not ability, but availability. It is best to leave to Jesus the decision of who is fit to serve him. For his plans and purposes extend far beyond our limited range of vision. He gave his life for every one of us – and if you have decided to follow him, then he has already chosen you as being fit to serve.

For further reflection

1 Be still for a while. Allow God to grant you his peace in the stillness.

2 Listen to or sing a song or hymn which encapsulates the message of the cross. How do you feel about this amazing love which Jesus demonstrated? Turn your thoughts into prayer.

3 Ask God to bring a fresh sense of calling into your own life, to be the bearer of his good news.

A prayer

Lord, receive my life as an offering.
You have shown me greater love than I could ever return.
Receive my life: my heart, my mind, my hands, my lips.
Take me and use me.

As you were sent, so send me:
With grace and truth to speak the love of God.
Compel me with that same love
into the world to share your good news.
In Jesus' name. Amen.

Day 20 (Friday)

Mission Impossible?

'It is I myself!'
(Luke 24.39)

Today we focus our attention on the nature of the instructions which God gives us to serve him. What will it mean for us?

'"As the Father has sent me, I am sending you"' – that was how Jesus described the way in which the disciples would go in his name. At this point I can imagine them feeling they had just been volunteered for Mission Impossible. The people of Israel at the time of Moses must have felt a similar wave of trepidation as they listened to the way God intended them to live for him. Notice how Moses reassured them:

> Now what I am commanding you today is not too difficult for you or beyond your reach. It is not up in heaven, so that you have to ask, 'Who will ascend into heaven to get it and proclaim it to us so that we may obey it?' Nor is it beyond the sea, so that you have to ask, 'Who will cross the sea to get it and proclaim it to us so that we may obey it?' No, the word is very near you.
>
> (Deuteronomy 30.11–14)

Jesus could have spoken the same words to his disciples when they first began to follow him. He was not calling them to a way of life completely alien to them: they had followed in his footsteps during the years they had spent with him. He had given them a model. The disciples had the opportunity to scrutinize Jesus' life closely. Although

Jesus had his moments of privacy, he consistently allowed his words and actions to be plainly heard and seen. Such was his example. He wanted to leave an indelible impression on them. On page after page in the Gospels we see insights of Jesus' public and private life, clearly recorded.

"'As the Father has sent me, I am sending you.'" What an encouragement to know that it is Jesus himself who sends us out. Have you ever been under the direction of someone who did not inspire you with confidence at all? Perhaps you've struggled with a teacher who had neither the command of their subject, nor the ability to convey it. The result is a lack of understanding on your part, and little sense of being empowered to work at things on your own.

How different it is with Jesus. Just imagine what would have come of his disciples if Jesus had said to them something like, 'Well, guys, thanks for coming along with me these last few years. We've had some good times, haven't we? Now it's time for you to make a go of it yourselves. But look, don't worry too much how you go about it. If it looks OK and feels fine, then I'm sure things will work out for you.' In contrast Jesus led by example, to show that it matters what you do and say.

We can have full confidence in our guide and instructor. So vital was it to Jesus that his disciples fully grasped that confidence in him, that he gave them a repeat performance of his Emmaus road Bible study. Cleopas and his friend saw the afternoon matinée; the others now had a chance to hear the evening performance. He opened their minds to understand all that was spoken about him in the Scriptures.

"'Why do doubts rise in your minds?'" Jesus asked them. He had quizzed them with this same question after he had calmed the storm. On that occasion they had wondered in whose company they were. Now they were grasping a whole new dimension of the enormity of who Jesus really was. He was back from the dead. They were realizing that they were in the presence of someone quite awesome. They were being invited to touch the skin of God incarnate.

Because it is he who sends us, our calling is far from being Mission Impossible, but is brought within the bounds of plausibility. For it's not just anyone who's doing the calling. Jesus stood among his bewildered disciples and said, "'It is I myself!'" He needed no other introduction. He was his very own definition.

For further reflection

List some of Jesus' character-qualities. How could each of these encourage you as you step out to live for him? How do these give you confidence in the one who is sending you out?

A prayer

Lord, it's so good to know that it's you who sends me out.
You call me to serve you;
help me to be ready.
Thank you that you not only call me,
but also equip me for mission.
Fill me with your Holy Spirit
and send me out in your power. Amen.

Day 21

꧁ꕥ꧂

Not in our own strength

And with this he breathed on them and said, 'Receive
the Holy Spirit.'

(John 20.22)

It was not what the disciples expected, to have Jesus
breathe on them. Mind you, for most of that momentous
day, they had been encountering the unexpected as if it
was commonplace. What must the first disciples have felt
at this point? For the breath of Jesus upon them was so
much more than just a physical occurrence, ruffling their
hair and stroking their skin. Here was the very life of God,
in the person of the Holy Spirit, coming to infuse them.
There was a deep stirring within each disciple, giving rise
to the dawn of a new confidence. Here was Jesus preparing them for a great task.

Jesus' preparation was always meticulous. When it came
to a task, he always laid a careful plan of campaign to
ensure that all would be properly attended to. If Jesus
made such meticulous arrangements for the Last Supper
(Mark 14.12–16), how much more would he have prepared the way for his disciples to share his good news with
all people?

Following his resurrection, before Jesus sent out his
disciples, he conferred on them his Holy Spirit. This was
not the main outpouring of the Spirit which came at
Pentecost, following the ascension. This was recognition
that, even in those early days of being equipped for
service, with Jesus appearing to them, they still needed
the power of the Spirit at work in their lives. If the
disciples needed him then, even with Jesus around,

how much more do we need his presence in our lives today?

The Holy Spirit is to evangelism what petrol is to the car engine. The Spirit is the empowerer, enlightener and energizer in the task of spreading the good news.

Jesus knew how important it was for the disciples to be empowered by the Spirit for the work he was calling them to. In the upper room that Easter evening, he conferred on them an initial gift of the Spirit. But a fuller measure of that gift was coming later.

"'I am going to send you what my Father has promised; but stay in the city until you have been clothed with power from on high'" (Luke 24.49). The word 'clothed' in the original Greek means 'to put on' in the sense of getting dressed. So Jesus was saying that his disciples needed to be dressed up with the Spirit. It was important for them to wait for this empowering. They were not yet fully equipped. Astronauts do not go for a space-walk unless they are wearing a full spacesuit. Divers do not jump into the sea unless they have the right breathing apparatus, flippers and masks. In the same way, Jesus was telling his followers that they must be clothed in the right way to be effective in ministry.

The Holy Spirit is indispensable to all of us as we seek to live for the Lord. At certain times there are particular tasks to which God will call us, which will require special training. Some friends of mine have just left to serve for two years on a missionary ship. In obedience to God's call they have already been through some rigorous selection procedures, and now embark on several more weeks of preparation and orientation before they finally board the ship. This enforced period of waiting has at times been difficult for them. There has sometimes been an overwhelming feeling of wanting to get on with it. Such times of preparation can prove trying – however, with hindsight we do see the value of them. The disciples may well have found their own waiting phase frustrating and difficult. They were instructed to wait in Jerusalem, the place of their greatest failure and shame, the place where their enemies were closest. But even there Jesus promised to send his power through the Spirit.

And Jesus kept that promise. At Pentecost we see the full outpouring of the Spirit for the work of the gospel. Many times in Acts we read of the apostles operating in the power of the Spirit (for example, Acts 2.4; 4.8; 4.31; 7.55). For the early apostles, the Spirit and evangelism were inseparable. How sad it is, then, that we reduce this sovereign work of God purely to techniques, methodologies and programmes. Our 'experience' can make God redundant if it makes us think we have all the answers. Such mentality fails to understand the truth that no one can come to Jesus unless drawn by the Father through the Spirit.

One immediate corollary of operating in the power of the Spirit is given by Jesus' words: '"If you forgive anyone their sins, they are forgiven; if you do not forgive them, they are not forgiven"'. The Spirit is the *Holy* Spirit, who convicts the world of sin and unrighteousness (John 16.8). Lives governed by the Holy Spirit are shocked by unholiness. Part of our calling is to expose such things while releasing the power of forgiveness in Jesus' name to those who are repentant. This is a tremendous responsibility, but one which is at the heart of the very gospel we seek to share. And what a privilege it is to see someone who turns away from sin to accept Christ's lordship and his salvation.

The Apostle Paul urged us to 'be filled with the Spirit' (Ephesians 5.18). He used the present continuous tense in this phrase, implying we should be seeking continually to be filled. It is not just a once-for-all experience at conversion. We need a daily fresh outpouring.

For further reflection

1 Invite the Holy Spirit into your life today. Welcome his presence in as many specific areas of your life as come to mind. Ask for his power to be at work in you.

2 Pray for wisdom, sensitivity and courage to confront unrighteousness and injustice. Where are you aware of these around you at the moment?

A prayer

Breathe on me, Breath of God;
Fill me with life anew,
That I would love what thou dost love,
And do what thou wouldst do.

(Edwin Hatch, 1835–99)

The Upper Room Revisited

Now Thomas (called Didymus), one of the Twelve, was not with the disciples when Jesus came. So the other disciples told him, 'We have seen the Lord!'

But he said to them, 'Unless I see the nail marks in his hands and put my finger where the nails were, and put my hand into his side, I will not believe it.'

A week later his disciples were in the house again, and Thomas was with them. Though the doors were locked, Jesus came and stood among them and said, 'Peace be with you!' Then he said to Thomas, 'Put your finger here; see my hands. Reach out your hand and put it into my side. Stop doubting and believe.'

Thomas said to him, 'My Lord and my God!'

Then Jesus told him, 'Because you have seen me, you have believed; blessed are those who have not seen and yet have believed.'

(John 20.24–9)

Day 22 (Sunday)

❧❧❧

The man who wasn't there

Now Thomas ... was not with the disciples when Jesus came.

(John 20.24)

One of the mysteries surrounding that first Easter Day is the whereabouts of Thomas on that momentous evening when Jesus appeared to the disciples. Why was he not there?

We all like to pass our judgement on 'doubting Thomas' – we even label others by the same name if they show signs of wavering over some issue. Could it not be, however, that we have not grasped the seriousness of Thomas' situation? Was he suffering some kind of faith crisis of which the others were unaware? Were the others not looking out for him? They had always been prone to looking after their own interests.

This incident brings into focus the whole issue of how we look out for the spiritual well-being of others. We live with unprecedented pressures and demands, and we all need to be careful we do not fall. It is tragic to hear stories of those we know who were once Christians, but have now left the Church and their Christian way of life, through experiencing a severe crisis of faith.

Such stories leave us numb, questioning the stability of our own faith. There may be many factors affecting those who have left the Church, and their decision may have been precipitated by the most difficult personal circumstances. It is not for us to judge. But it should focus our attention more sharply on looking out for each other's well-being. It is tragic that this subject of conversation has become taboo in many Christian circles. We don't like to ask people how they are getting on in their faith because we feel it may be too personal, a bit like not wanting to inquire why someone is going to the doctor's. How sad that we have lost touch with talking to others about the health of their relationship with God.

When I was a young Christian in my teens, our church youth-group held regular evenings where all those who were active Christians would talk for a few minutes about how they were getting on with God. The discipline of attending these meetings was sometimes difficult – they were more serious than some of our other get-togethers. But looking back I am now immensely grateful for these meetings, because they gave us a forum within which to talk openly about our joys and struggles in the Christian life. These evenings provided our youth-group leaders with an accurate thermometer with which to test the spiritual temperature of the group members. Those people who consistently absented themselves from these meetings, and yet attended all the others, became a cause for concern. Our leaders had a valuable early sign that something may have been wrong.

Having been privileged to work for a mission agency, committed to communicating the relevance of the Christian faith, I have seen many people becoming Christians for the first time, and others making recommitments, indicating that at some time in the past they have slipped back from a fully committed Christian life. I expect most of us can think of someone we know who used to be an active Christian, but who no longer seems committed to the Lord.

How good are we at looking out for the spiritual well-being of other Christians? As we begin to listen to, and share with, each other, it brings a sense of accountability and deepens the trust we place in our Christian friends. It allows us to support and pray for one another; we will hold each other in our hearts.

It might shock us if we knew just how many Christians are breaking apart inwardly, and yet have not been able to share this with anyone else. They may be disintegrating on the inside, and yet their plight is unknown. We were not made to live in isolation; we need to cultivate interdependence with our Christian brothers and sisters. Whom can we take under our wing today? Whom will we speak to if we ourselves are in need?

For further reflection

1 Pray for anyone you know who is experiencing a difficult time in their faith. Be open as to how you may be able to help them.

2 Consider seriously if you should link up with a few others to form a prayer group, within which you will each have the opportunity to talk openly about your joys and struggles in your faith. You may already belong to a house group where you can do this – but if not, consider finding some others with whom you can pray regularly.

A prayer

Lord, help me to look out for the spiritual needs of others.
Draw me from the cocoon of my own self-interest.
May I rejoice with those who rejoice
and weep with those who weep,
possessing your heart of compassion and empathy
for those who need help.
In Jesus' name. Amen.

Day 23 (Monday)

Holding on to faith

> Now Thomas ... was not with the disciples when Jesus
> came.
>
> (John 20.24)

The Bible gives us plenty of insights into the plight of
those who, like Thomas, suffer a crisis of faith. In his first
letter to Timothy, Paul writes 'I give you this instruction in
keeping with the prophecies once made about you, so that
by following them you may fight the good fight, holding
on to faith and a good conscience. Some have rejected
these and so have shipwrecked their faith' (1 Timothy
1.18–19).

A shipwreck of faith – what a dramatic picture. Yet this
is no empty analogy – this is a verbal picture painted out
of raw experience. Paul had lived through three ship-
wrecks and spent a day and a night in the open sea (2
Corinthians 11.25). In his mind's eye he could see the
devastation of a ship lost at sea. He knew the dangers of
submerged rocks, the unpredictability of strong currents,
the power of a freak storm. How fitting that he should use
such a word to describe what some people experience
when they lose their faith. It must feel as if elemental
forces are unleashed against you. Thomas was in that
storm. The darkness of Good Friday still enveloped him, a
biting wind of grief tore into him, waves of doubt broke
over him. The mast of his life was under supreme strain,
the rigging was flailing, the sails in tatters. Thomas was
heading for the rocks.

But hope was on hand for him, as we shall see in the
next few days. Paul, too, offers us advice on how we can

hold on to faith. What can we do when circumstances assault our soul and threaten to overwhelm us? What can we do to help others we know are in this position? In 1 Timothy 1.12–19, we find four ways to tighten our grip on faith.

1 REMEMBER HOW GOD HAS BROUGHT YOU ON

Paul recounts his story of conversion. He is especially conscious of how far the Lord has brought him – blasphemer to believer; from persecutor to proclaimer. For us, the story may not be so dramatic, but for those who seek to follow Christ, the marks of his lordship will be upon us; the landmarks of our journey are there to guide us. They shine out like lighthouses, warning us of the rocks where we may run aground. We know where we used to be; we see where, by God's grace, we are now. And a voyage of grace it is, a journey full of the mercy of God. All this is evidence of his activity in our lives. This brings me to the next point.

2 GOD HAS APPOINTED US

He considers us worthy of service in his kingdom, where no one is unemployed. God asks us instead to sign up to serve him as Lord. He has a job for all of us – we need not fear rejection or feel useless.

3 REMEMBER WHAT GOD HAS PROMISED YOU IN THE PAST

At various times in his past, Timothy had received prophecies through which God had spoken to him directly. Paul reminds Timothy of these as a further encouragement to establish him firmly in his faith. Paul himself had heard God's voice in the past, and in his preaching he mentioned the way in which God had spoken (Acts 22.6–11; 26.12–18). For Paul, one firm support for his faith was the knowledge of God's words to him – and what dependable words they were. We may not feel that God has spoken directly to us in this way –

however, through his word, the Bible, he speaks and guides. 'Your word is a lamp to my feet and a light for my path' (Psalm 119.105).

4 REMEMBER YOUR CONSCIENCE

Paul tells Timothy that holding on to faith also means holding on to a good conscience, which gives a foundation to faith. Notice that Paul says it must be a good conscience. Our consciences will be corrupted if we choose to undermine the place they have in our hearts. Devalue them and they will deceive you, as the line between right and wrong begins to move and wrong gains the upper hand.

These four pointers are all encouragements we could use to help those we know who are struggling in their faith. They may prove to be the lifeboats that reach the foundering ship of their faith and rescue it from the destruction of the storm. The Christian life is not plain sailing all the time, but in his grace God has provided these ways to steady our position and protect us from the storms of life.

For further reflection

1 Review a situation which concerns you in the light of the four points given above. How do these help you to gain a fuller perspective of the situation? Bring these thoughts honestly to the Lord in prayer. If you are able, ask someone else to pray for you also.

2 Pray again for the person you thought of yesterday who is struggling in their faith. Could any of the points in today's chapter be helpful for them?

A prayer

Father, I praise you that as I look back,
I realize how you have led me on.
Father, I am not all that I wish to be,
yet by your grace I am not what I used to be.

Thank you for choosing me.
Tighten your grip on my life,
that I would be held strong and true,
protected from the storms which assault my soul.
For Jesus' sake. Amen.

Day 24 (Tuesday)

Have you heard the good news?

'Stop doubting and believe.'
(John 20.27b)

So far we have taken time to think through some of the issues which Thomas may have faced on that first Easter evening. His own crisis of faith led him that night to dismiss the testimony of the other ten apostles – he refused to believe their story. He had not seen Jesus himself; he wanted more proof of his resurrection than just the word of others. After all, he might have thought, it's easy to deceive yourself into believing the reality of something you hope for, even if it's not yet come true. All the disciples wished Jesus wasn't dead. How easy it would have been to talk themselves into believing that the cross was just a bad dream and that Jesus was still alive. 'No,' Thomas declared, 'I will not believe your story.'

John's narrative now gives us a tantalizing interlude of a whole week. We have no details as to what the disciples did during that time. It is clear that there were no new resurrection appearances to these disciples in this period, as Jesus' entrance into the upper room a week later was the next opportunity for them to see him – and Thomas was still doubting up till then. It must have been a strange week; Thomas would have been a black sheep among the others. Did they recount their first encounter with Jesus again during that week? I'm sure they didn't keep quiet about it! How did Thomas feel as he no doubt overheard these conversations? Maybe he continued openly to proclaim his disbelief in their story. It raises questions as to how we behave in the presence of unbelievers. I hope the other disciples did not take on a high-and-mighty attitude. Were they sensitive to Thomas?

A week later Thomas got his opportunity to meet Jesus. But not only did he meet the risen Jesus, he also met the rebuking Christ. For Jesus' chastisement was not just a matter of Thomas lacking faith in him – Thomas had also lacked faith in his friends in failing to believe their testimony. Jesus calls us into fellowship with other Christians. We need to have encouragements from them by hearing what the Lord is doing in their lives. To dismiss someone's testimony is not only to demean the one who was blessed, but it also devalues the God who blesses.

Have you ever listened to someone recounting how God has done something in their life, and not really believed it? I have caught myself on a number of occasions thinking such sceptical thoughts as, 'I'm sure their healing is due to the fact that it was probably all psychosomatic in the first place,' or, 'They say they've become a Christian, but I know what they've been like and I don't reckon it will last long'. May God deliver me from such a critical spirit in the future. Of course we need to look for genuine cases of God at work, but how easily we can dismiss someone's story, particularly when it has not been our experience. This was the case for Thomas: *he* hadn't seen Jesus alive, so why should he believe the others?

In his grace God deals with all of us as individuals, and works in our lives accordingly. He longs for us to welcome all that he is doing in other people. In his letter to the Galatian church, Paul is thrilled to tell of the churches in Judaea, who did not know him at all and yet fully received the news of his conversion. 'They only heard the report, "The man who formerly persecuted us is now preaching the faith he once tried to destroy." And they praised God because of me' (Galatians 1.23–4). 'They only heard the report …' – what a great example. To those Christians, hearing was believing. They did not need to meet Paul. They gladly welcomed the news about what God had done, and gave him the glory. In his rebuke of Thomas,

Jesus was calling him and us to behave in the same way as those Judaean Christians.

Thomas's disbelief in that week after the first Easter Day reminds us of the elder brother in Jesus' parable of the Prodigal Son. For in that classic story we have another example of someone who refused to believe good news. It was a story of two sons: the prodigal and the petulant. There is no containing the father's joy on the prodigal's return. The son is treated to quite a homecoming: best robe, ring, sandals, fattened calf, sumptuous feast, music, dancing. The whole household is inside celebrating – all except one. The elder brother won't come in. There he is sulking outside the house, back turned, arms crossed. His father's pleadings for him to come inside are drowned, just as much by his own refusal to listen as by the sound of the celebrations. The elder brother is unmoved by the mercy shown to his returning brother. He is appalled at the extravagance of the party. He sulks at his own misfortunes. He has lost the capacity to receive good news.

The tragedy of that parable is that the story ends with the elder brother still outside. He missed the celebrations. He missed the good news. And for that week after that first Easter Thomas missed receiving the blessing of the most wonderful news there has ever been. All because he did not accept the testimony of his friends.

Let us not sit in the company of Thomas or the elder brother. Let us humbly acknowledge the God who works in each person according to his sovereign purpose, and rejoice in all that he does to bless others.

For further reflection

1 Confess to God any times you can remember when you have dismissed a genuine testimony shared by someone. Ask God to give you a more receptive heart to receive such news in future.

2 Seek to encourage someone in the next week by telling them of something the Lord has done for you.

A prayer

Father, I am so grateful for all that you have done in my life.

Help me to have a wider vision of all that you are doing in others also.

Make me a receiver of good news as well as a giver of it.

In Jesus' name. Amen.

Day 25 (Wednesday)

A reconditioned faith

'Because you have seen me, you have believed.'
(John 20.29)

Sweeping across Germany at the end of World War II, allied forces searched farms and houses looking for snipers. At one abandoned house which was almost a heap of rubble, searchers with flashlights found their way to the basement. There on the crumbling wall a victim of the Holocaust had scratched a star of David and beneath it in rough lettering the inscription:

I believe in the sun even when it does not shine,
I believe in love even when it is not shown,
I believe in God even when he does not speak.

Here indeed was faith. The suffering endured by the writer of those words cannot be imagined. For him or her, God seemed absent and silent. And yet faith prevailed.

This was the kind of faith that Jesus expected of Thomas – a faith which was not dependent on what is tangibly seen around us and experienced by us. The world's most famous doubter was, however, going to need convincing. Because for Thomas, seeing was believing. After the horrifying events of Good Friday, Thomas was living in a world where God seemed silent. It was the voice of black despair which clamoured louder than any other. And living under such conditions can have detrimental effects on our faith. The darkness of Thomas' own world caused him to adopt a 'preconditioned' faith – a cautious belief which placed conditions on the God he was to trust. It is a preconditioned faith which says, like

Thomas, 'Unless I ... then I will not believe'. Thomas needed a physically tangible sign of Jesus' presence. Something he could literally grasp with his hands and see with his eyes.

Jesus' rebuke of Thomas was not just for his inability to accept the testimony of others; it was also for his failure to possess a faith which saw beyond the physical.

'"Blessed are those who have not seen and yet have believed."' Jesus was saying that those with faith in him will have long-range vision to take them beyond their circumstances.

'We live by faith, not by sight,' wrote Paul to the Corinthian church (2 Corinthians 5.7). How do we mature in this kind of faith? It is a question of perspective. The resurrection sheds a new light on how we see life. We need to be daily discerning God's perspective on our circumstances in that resurrection light – for in that light, our predicaments take on less threatening dimensions. In 2 Corinthians 4 Paul tells us of his many struggles: 'Hard pressed on every side ... perplexed ... struck down' (8–9) – but viewed from God's eternal standpoint, these become to Paul but 'momentary troubles' (17). How, except in God's light, could we ever view such things in that way? What a difference it makes when we shift the focus of how we view our circumstances.

We can best develop a godly perspective through daily immersion in God's word, by letting this penetrate deep down to affect our thoughts and actions. This inner transformation to adopting God's values turns our preconditioned faith into a reconditioned one.

We may well be mocked by others as we seek to share our faith, and live for God. The modern world prides itself on advancement through knowledge: as believers we may well be considered as blind by those who champion the cause of science or the intellect. But as our world becomes increasingly dark, it is those who are deemed blind who will see the best. The story is told of a blind girl called Nydia who lived in the ancient city of

Pompeii. She was often ridiculed by others as she struggled to make a living selling flowers on the street. One day Mount Vesuvius erupted nearby, sending plumes of black soot so thickly into the air that the sun was blocked out. It happened so suddenly and unexpectedly that there was no time for lamps to be lit: the whole city became engulfed in darkness. Scattering wildly, the people fled to and fro, groping blindly to escape the city as tons of molten lava poured down into the streets and houses. Many failed to escape, lost in the darkness. Yet others were saved, as Nydia led hundreds of them to safety. Her expert knowledge of the city by touch alone allowed her to guide a group of frightened people to safe territory. In the darkness her blindness became the means for other people to see.

How much more we will save others by living according to a reconditioned faith that disregards the 'unless …' mentality? For attempting to view life from God's perspective helps us look beyond our present circumstances and brings distant hopes within grasp. This is the way that life was viewed by that Jewish prisoner during the Holocaust. The darkness of the situation did not stop them believing in God, even when he seemed absent. For the vision of faith, just like Nydia's, penetrates much darkness. Does your faith need a reconditioning?

For further reflection

1 Are you aware of any situations in your life where you have placed God in a box, by telling him how you want him to act? How could the way Jesus dealt with Thomas affect this way of thinking?

2 If God has seemed silent and far away recently, allow this story to encourage you. Jesus was very much alive during the week following his resurrection, even if Thomas did not feel this to be true. Ask God to open your eyes to see him at work, even at this difficult time.

A prayer

Father, help me to see more and more
that you are greater than I could ever imagine,
that you have plans for me which are better than I could
    ever perceive,
and that the way in which you work is always the best.
Reshape my thinking, re-order my mind by your Holy
    Spirit,
so that I have a view of you which is accurate.
Father, recondition my faith. In Jesus' name. Amen.

Day 26 (Thursday)

Faith to see beyond our generation

'Blessed are those who have not seen and yet have believed.'

(John 20.29b)

When Jesus challenged Thomas to walk by faith, not by sight, he was commending to him the example of many great people of faith from the Old Testament. In Hebrews 11 the writer presents us with a gallery of characters who all displayed this one common characteristic: they believed God's purposes, even when they did not see the fulfilment of the final goal.

Scan your eye along this gallery of faithful people. Take Noah for example: he'd never seen a flood – or an ark for that matter – yet God asked him to build the ark to save his family from the flood. God's ultimate goal – to provide a new world free from the former wickedness – was only seen by Noah towards the end of his life.

Abraham followed the way of faith also. Uprooted from his family home, he was led to a country of which he had no previous knowledge. He lived there only as a stranger, yet God promised to give that whole land to his descendants as their final home. Wizened and frail, he was promised a son as the first of those descendants. He believed God and saw the fulfilment of that first stage of God's plan. But Abraham saw nothing of the fuller picture of the whole Israelite nation made up of his descendants.

The writer of Hebrews makes the following comment about these people: 'These people were still living by faith when they died. They did not receive the things promised; they only saw them and welcomed them from a distance' (Heb 11.13).

God had revealed a big picture to both Noah and Abraham – like giving them a trailer for a film. Yet neither of them would live to see the film itself, or how it would end. They had to understand that they each had a vital part to play in God's purposes, but that they would not see the final fulfilment in their own lifetime. Noah built a boat and Abraham fathered a son, so that God could create a nation, set apart for himself. Noah and Abraham served God's purposes in their own generation, in order that greater purposes would be fulfilled in generations to come. King David is also commended as someone who acted like this (see Acts 13.36). They are all examples of people who lived to the full in their own generation, but were always aware of the future.

This is why Jesus challenged Thomas to walk by faith – and that's why he calls us to do the same. Jesus knew that as the disciples shared the gospel they would start the most wonderful chain-reaction the world has ever known. The gospel has been faithfully handed down to each generation since the news first broke. The first disciples only caught a glimpse of God's great plan to bring the gospel to all the nations, but they knew where to start – and for them that was sufficient. They gave their utmost to the Lord within their own lifetime, without knowing fully the wonderful scale of God's plan of salvation.

How far-sighted is our faith? Do we get discouraged because we feel that our contribution is so minimal as to be negligible? Underestimation of the future fruitfulness of our faith will diminish our enthusiasm to continue in our God-given tasks. As we walk in God's way for us, we can all make a difference because we all have a role. As we seek to live for God we become part of that great line of faithful people who are praised in the letter to the Hebrews. And in our actions and words we can be laying down examples for others to follow.

For further reflection

1 However insignificant you feel you are, thank God that you play an important role in his great plan. Reaffirm your desire to serve him.

2 Pray for at least one senior Church leader, that God would strengthen and guide them as they live out their vision, which may affect great numbers of people both today and in future years.

A prayer

Father, I want to serve your purposes in my generation.
But I also want to make a difference for you which will last longer.
Raise my expectations of you;
open my eyes to see where I may serve you in ways that will touch other people.
Make me a catalyst of change for the extension of your Kingdom. Amen.

A Breakfast on the Beach

Afterwards Jesus appeared again to his disciples, by the Sea of Tiberias. It happened this way: Simon Peter, Thomas (called Didymus), Nathaniel from Cana in Galilee, the sons of Zebedee, and two other disciples were together. 'I'm going out to fish,' Simon Peter told them, and they said, 'We'll go with you.' So they went out and got into the boat, but that night they caught nothing.

Early in the morning, Jesus stood on the shore, but the disciples did not realize that it was Jesus.

He called out to them, 'Friends, haven't you any fish?'

'No,' they answered.

He said, 'Throw your net on the right side of the boat and you will find some.' When they did, they were unable to haul the net in because of the large number of fish.

Then the disciple whom Jesus loved said to Peter, 'It is the Lord!' As soon as Simon Peter heard him say, 'It is the Lord,' he wrapped his outer garment around him (for he had taken it off) and jumped into the water. The other disciples followed in the boat, towing the net full of fish, for they were not far from shore, about a hundred yards. When they landed, they saw a fire of burning coals there with fish on it, and some bread.

Jesus said to them, 'Bring some of the fish you have just caught.'

Simon Peter climbed aboard and dragged the net ashore. It was full of fish, 153, but even with so many the net was not torn. Jesus said to them, 'Come and have breakfast.' None of the disciples dared ask him, 'Who are you?' They knew it was the Lord. Jesus came, took the bread and gave it to them, and did the same with the fish. This was now the third time Jesus appeared to his disciples after he was raised from the dead.

When they had finished eating, Jesus said to Simon Peter, 'Simon son of John, do you truly love me more than these?'

'Yes, Lord,' he said, 'you know that I love you.'

Jesus said, 'Feed my lambs.'

Again Jesus said, 'Simon son of John, do you truly love me?'

He answered, 'Yes, Lord, you know that I love you.'

Jesus said, 'Take care of my sheep.'

The third time he said to him, 'Simon son of John, do you love me?'

Peter was hurt because Jesus asked him the third time, 'Do you love me?' He said, 'Lord, you know all things; you know that I love you.'

Jesus said, 'Feed my sheep.' …

Peter turned and saw that the disciple whom Jesus loved was following them … When Peter saw him, he asked, 'Lord, what about him?'

Jesus answered, 'If I want him to remain alive until I return, what is that to you? You must follow me.'

(John 21.1–17, 20–22)

Day 27 (Friday)

Stuck in old ways?

'I'm going out to fish.'
(John 21.3)

You're the centre of activity among your peers. If there's anything worth doing, then you're the one to do it. Perhaps you're not so hot on thinking things through beforehand though. Your motto has tended to be: Act now, think later. Great for those moments when seconds count and decisive leadership is what matters most; not so good, however, for those times when brash bravado leads you into more trouble. Like those incidents of sword-wielding in an olive grove and of firelight conversations in the high priest's courtyard which do not seem that long ago …

Who are you? Well, that's an interesting question. Three years ago, you could have answered that question very simply. You are Simon, the son of John. Fisherman by trade and fiery by nature. There were not many people who messed with you – and those who did felt the full force of your fiery temperament. That was until the day when Jesus met you and changed the course of your life. He was the only person with whom you felt you had met your match. And with Jesus it was more a case of game, set and match to him. He'd won you over and chose to call you Peter, the Rock. You embraced your new name with delight. 'The Rock; yes that's me: strong, solid, dependable. A born leader.' You'd keep those other disciples in check. In fact, you had a good mind to take on the Romans, too. They'd been pushing around the Jewish people for too long, and with Jesus about to usurp them and become king – well, you certainly wanted to be right in the thick of the action.

But everything's different now. Even after you have met the risen Jesus, you still don't feel like you used to. And you're not quite sure if you're Peter anymore. You certainly don't feel like that Rock. Painful memories of the last few weeks still come back to you – memories that make you realize you've acted more like the old Simon, rather than the person Jesus intended you to be. Perhaps you should have seen the warning signs. Jesus even began using your old name at the Last Supper, and alerting you to the dangers ahead. But you didn't heed the warnings; you fell from grace in a big way and you are now suffering from an identity crisis. Will Jesus ever trust you again to be the Peter he wanted you to be?

And to make matters worse, there's all this waiting. If there's one thing you'd never win prizes for, it's waiting. You never queue for anything. Patience is certainly a virtue, but it's not really one of yours – you are a got-to-be-up-and-doing sort of person. It's been a while since any of you last saw Jesus – and the last thing he said to you was wait. Wait for the gift of the Father. But nothing has happened yet and you've started to get itchy feet. You feel you have to *do* something. Surely it must be time to *do* something?

And so you said you were going fishing. Don't look so surprised; at times like this a man has to act on instinct. And a fisherman's instinct is to fish. When there's nothing left to do, fishing seemed as good an option as anything else.

Or was it? It was not until the next morning that you realized the mistake you had made. Looking back, you can see that actually you were going back to old ways. Jesus had told you that he was making you fishers of men. The fishing boats that you had beached three years ago, were not due for a re-launch. You know now that Jesus meant that you were going to be doing new things. It was not that your fishing skills were of no value: it was more that Jesus was giving you a new job. Although Jesus sometimes employs past skills in a new ministry, this would not be true with your fishing. Looking back, you can see that it was a lesson well learned.

Yours was a lesson you urged all believers to learn from when you later wrote, 'We should not live the rest of our earthly lives for evil human desires, but rather for the will of God, for we have spent enough time in the past doing what pagans choose to do' (1 Peter 4.2–3, author's paraphrase).

For further reflection

1 Identify one aspect of your life that still seems to retain characteristics of your old self – how you were before you became a Christian, which was not in line with Christ's teaching. Invite the Holy Spirit to come afresh into this area and transform it.

2 Explore some practical ways of demonstrating that you have chosen to leave those old ways behind (for example, if you have experienced problems with gossiping, try to take more opportunities to build others up with your words). Ask God to strengthen and establish this new habit.

3 If you are going through a time of reflection in your life, waiting for something new to begin, ask the Lord for patience and determination to seek him for his direction.

A prayer

Lord, I have spent too much time on things which do not matter.
I have whiled away precious moments, acting in old habits from which you have called me.
Lord, I am sorry for the times when I've gone back to those things,

when I have not responded to the new challenges of faith.
Help me to look forward.
You have called me for a purpose.
Help me to embrace it
for your glory's sake. Amen.

Day 28 (Saturday)

The dangers of old ways

So they went out into the boat, but that night they caught nothing.

(John 21.3)

Yesterday we placed ourselves in the shoes of Simon Peter, and discovered some of the thoughts and emotions which he might have been experiencing as this next resurrection appearance unfolds. Simon Peter probably typified the disciples as a whole during this period of waiting – a phase of inactivity seemed difficult for them to handle. And so the temptation to be doing something, even if it was returning to old ways, became very real.

In this story we see several dangers which result from falling back into old patterns of behaviour. The first is that our own decision to lapse can affect other people. Notice how Peter's declaration to go fishing did not actually mention the other disciples. It was not, 'Let's all go fishing'. Instead he declared '*I'm* going fishing'. He was simply stating his own personal preference, yet his actions took all the others with him. For those who don't know what else to do, it can be very attractive to follow someone else who displays some kind of leadership. And so all those disciples ended up in the same boat, literally. It is wise for us to be aware of our responsibility to others in this respect. No one is an island when it comes to behaviour. There are people watching us; our words and actions influence those around us; our conduct is important. What signals are we giving? Where are we leading people? 'We put no stumbling block in anyone's path,' wrote Paul in 2 Corinthians 6.3. He was very conscious of his own responsibility to live a life that could be an example to others.

The disciples laboured all night with their nets and came up with nothing. They fished at the best time, with good equipment. They had the necessary skills and they knew the lake well – but still they caught nothing. Tired and weary by the first light of day, they see a figure on the distant shore. It's Jesus, but they don't recognize him. Once before, when the disciples had struggled while out on the lake, Jesus had come close to help them This time he remained on the shore. He was very much on the fringe of their activity – and that's what it's like when we slip back into old ways. He'll seem a distant figure; we may not even recognize his presence at all. We will lose that closeness for which he longs.

Jesus may seem distant at times like this, but be assured that he has not gone completely. In fact, he is surveying the results of your labours back in the old way of things. Jesus looked out over the water at his disciples and saw the frustrated faces, tired bodies and empty nets that spoke of an unfruitful night. The futility of their actions had been revealed, and Jesus was on hand to make them fully realize this.

"'Haven't you any fish?'" he inquired across the water. Here is another one of those searching questions that the disciples had to answer during this 40-day period. For this question wasn't simply a query about facts and figures. When the disciples answered, "'No'" (and there was not much point in giving any other answer), it was more than just a statement of fact. Jesus' question was a probe into how worthwhile their whole night's activity had been. The emptiness of their nets testified to the barrenness of a life spent back in old ways, the unfruitfulness of living in a way which the Lord had called them from.

The Lord also surveys the results of our labours. Some of our actions are sadly like those of the disciples that night. We spend a lot of time and energy in activities we believe ourselves to be good at, and yet these things may belong to an old way of life from which the Lord has called us. What would we say to him if he questioned us about some of our behaviour and actions? '"Haven't you any fish?"' was his question to the disciples. For us, his challenge may be couched in other words:

'What good came out of that conversation on the telephone just now?'

'What have you got to show for yourself now that your day is over?'

It is not easy to face questions like these, but they certainly help us to focus on the fruitful rather than the futile. I am encouraged that Jesus challenged the disciples about their actions. It showed his passion for them to live lives that counted. His commitment to us hasn't changed either. He surveys our struggles and looks upon even our efforts which seem wasted – and he has an answer for us all. To the disciples he said, '"Throw your net on the right side of the boat"'. To us he will say, 'Try again; there's another way, you know. Don't give up. Yes, you've had a wasted time. But if you see how unproductive the old ways are, I can introduce you to ways that are new.'

The disciples realized that Jesus saw fish even when they couldn't. He knew how to turn empty nets into full ones. And he can speak into the barrenness of our old ways and set us on the right path.

For further reflection

1 Take some time over the next week to review and evaluate some of your actions and lifestyle. Does anything seem fruitless? If so, ask the Lord to show you whether these things do not belong to his new ways for you. What else may the Lord be saying to you through this?

2 Ask God to help you understand more fully his priorities for you, and to focus you on them, protecting you from possible distractions. It is good to remember that saying, 'No' to one thing may enable you to say, 'Yes' to something else.

A prayer

Lord Jesus, look with mercy on me
for the times when I have gone back to old ways
and spent times of fruitless labour which yielded nothing.
Forgive me.
Thank you that you have surveyed these unproductive
  efforts
and that you call me to better things.
Lead me into them and empower me to serve you afresh
  in the power of your Spirit. Amen.

Day 29 (Sunday)

───────────── ⌘ ─────────────

Turning point

No one dared ask him, 'Who are you?' They knew it was the Lord.

(John 21.12)

We have seen how the disciples had laboured fruitlessly for a whole night. We have watched Jesus survey the scene from the shore and speak to them across the water. Yet the disciples at that point did not recognize the Lord. In the early morning light, the figure was too distant to be clearly identifiable. And in their exhaustion and frustration with their worthless night's activity, the disciples would probably have listened to anyone giving them advice at this stage. And so they let their nets down on the other side of the boat.

Suddenly everything happens at once. There's movement in the net below. Cries echo back and forth from one end of the boat to the other. Men rush to the side. Arms strain to pull on the net. There are fish everywhere! Writhing, snapping at each other within the confines of the net, there seem too many to count. They are all beauties – a delight to the eyes of fishermen – a fine catch.

And then one cry cuts in above all the others. It is the voice of John – he was always the deep thinker, and for him the penny has dropped. He raises the cry, '"It is the Lord!"' He has forgotten the fish – something much more important has been discovered. It's *déjà vu*. The man on the shore has done this before. This was not the only fruitless night of fishing which had been transformed (see Luke 5.1–11). Once again empty nets had been filled.

John recognized Jesus acting in a way that was unmistakeably him. '"It is the Lord!"' rings out over the water. I can imagine all the other disciples' heads rising, temporarily distracted from the heaving net of fish beneath them. Only one person could turn things around in that way.

By the time Jesus had welcomed them to breakfast, John's realization of Jesus' identity had quickly spread among the disciples. We are told that all of them *knew* it was the Lord. All through the three years they had spent with Jesus, questions as to his real identity had dogged their steps. It was on that very lake, after a storm, that they had quizzed each other with terrified faces: "'Who is this, even the very wind and waves obey him?'" How fitting that in that same place they should become so convinced of the answer to that question.

This was a defining moment for them. All that they understood about Jesus had come together. They knew that Jesus had risen from the dead. They knew that he was Lord, even over death itself. But this realization had been a process. It is interesting to examine the Greek word used in the phrase, 'They knew it was the Lord'. It comes from the verb *oida*, which implies fullness of knowledge through experience. When John wrote, 'They knew it was the Lord', he was describing their certainty in recognizing the identity of Jesus.

Our understanding of what the Lord requires of us often unfolds as a process. It is a journey of faith. At each twist and turn we learn more about what it means to serve the Lord. At this juncture, it became clear to the disciples that Jesus really *was* serious about them leaving their fishing business behind. The disciples caught 153 fish that day; Jesus was now pointing them to the countless number of people who were still unsaved. This was to be the area of their ministry now – there was a catch of greater importance to land.

For further reflection

1 What things has Jesus done which have helped to convince you of his lordship? Praise him for these ways through which you have recognized him.

2 Pray for anyone you know who is not a Christian, that they may understand more fully the identity of God in Jesus Christ.

A prayer

Lord, I want to know you, really know you.
Not just something superficial or shallow,
but a relationship of depth and intimacy.
Open my eyes to see more of you.
Open my heart to receive more of you.
I know I've sometimes kept my distance.
Forgive me.
It's time to start again with a different goal.
Let's go deeper, Lord. Amen.

Day 30 (Monday)

Invitation to the great adventure

'Come and have breakfast.'
(John 21.12)

There's nothing like starting the day with a good breakfast. Even if you're a fisherman and you've worked hard all night, the stomach is just as much a priority as sleep. And when it's breakfast on the beach, well ... it's got to be quite tempting, hasn't it? For those early disciples that morning, the breakfast on offer was especially inviting. The charcoal was glowing and the smell of fish was very enticing. But the most welcoming aspect about this meal was the chef who bid them join him round the fire. God had built a barbecue on the beach.

'"Come and have breakfast,"' were his words of invitation. Those simple words so welcoming to the ears of tired and hungry men. I have a picture in my mind of that meal: it is of a remarkably relaxed occasion with servings of humour as generous of those of the fish. I can imagine lots of storytelling and good questions being asked of Jesus.

This is the last recorded time that Jesus invited them, '"Come ..."' – how fitting that it should be in this intimate setting of fellowship. For Jesus intended that intimacy to be more fully available through his Spirit which would be poured out following his ascension. But there had been other occasions when Jesus had used the word, '"Come"' – and each time it had been spoken, it had opened up a whole new vista of the life into which he was calling them.

First of all there was that tantalizing, '"Come and see"' that he uttered to two of John the Baptist's followers when they asked about him (John 1.39). It was an invitation to come closer in a non-threatening way, to make up their own minds about Jesus and to be involved in what he was doing. Jesus invites people to move towards God's way for them. How ready are we to respond to that call to check things out and learn more of what God is doing?

Then came perhaps the most famous invitation of all: the call to discipleship. "'Come, follow me'" (Mark 1.17), were the words of Jesus that day to the fishermen who were later to become his closest confidants. Three words which were destined to change the course of their lives forever. Leaving their nets, they obeyed the call. True discipleship cannot fail to change us too. We will certainly leave some things behind, for it will certainly involve a shedding of an old way of life, just like a snake sheds its old skin, in order to grow into the new life he has for us.

All these invitations may seem quite daunting at this stage. But just when this discipleship business might seem to be getting too much for us, Jesus gives us one of his most welcome invitations: "'Come to me, all you who are weary and burdened and I will give you rest'" (Matthew 11.28). Jesus does not require us to pick up the responsibilities of discipleship without providing us also with a place to leave the burdens of life – in his hands. We need not fear the pressures of life which sometimes crush us. Jesus' promise is that he can help us to carry them. His hands are big enough to receive them; his arms strong enough to bear them.

Safe in the knowledge of this depth of care, we as his disciples can step out in faith for him. Take Peter: he received one of the most scary invitations from Jesus that anyone had ever been given. We are back on the Sea of Galilee again, but this time we are in the middle of a storm. The disciples are fighting to keep their boat afloat – they are a long way from shore and tossed violently by the waves. Suddenly Jesus appears to them, walking on the water. Just the sight of him brought terror to the disciples – but a more frightening invitation is just coming up. At this point, Peter makes the most astonishing request: '"Lord, if it's you, tell me to come to you on the water."' That's quite a thing to ask when the lake is calm, let alone when there's a Force 9 gale blowing. Think twice before you ask such a thing of Jesus, for he may give you exactly what you ask for: '"Come,"' he said (Matthew 14.29). First Jesus told Peter to leave his nets, now he is asking him to leave his boat. This is the invitation to the great adventure, it is the invitation to step right out of the place you know is safe and to move into completely new territory.

Notice that this invitation from Jesus came only out of Peter's desire for it. His longing to know Christ deeply caused him to ask Jesus to lead him out on the water. And Jesus invited him to come. How prepared are we to ask God to take us on that great adventure? To take us beyond anything we have experienced? Will we ask him to give us fresh opportunities to live and speak for him? It's a risky thing to do, and it may be costly – but God honours those who step out in faith for him.

'"Come ..."' – a simple little word. Yet when it is spoken by Jesus a whole new dimension of life is opened for us. What will our response be to his invitation?

For further reflection

Bring your own response to the Lord for each of his invitations:

- To learn more about him: 'Come and see'.
- To leave our old ways of life to follow him: 'Come, follow me'.
- To leave our burdens with him: 'Come to me, all you who are burdened'.
- To step out in faith for him: 'Come'.

A prayer

Lord, you have always given the best invitations,
and I am drawn to accept.
You have held out your hands to me,
beckoning in love.
How can I resist, Lord?
How could I decline to come?
Lord, help me to say 'Yes' to you every time. Amen.

Day 31 (Tuesday)

On the scrap-heap?

'Simon, son of John, do you truly love me more than these?'

(John 21.15)

Have you ever felt like you were on the human scrap-heap? It's a dreadful place to be – a heartbreaking collection of the also-rans of life. These are people who have either been discarded by society as failures or who wrote themselves off years ago because of low self-esteem. They are dented by discouragement and crumpled by cares. This is a dead-end destination. They do not expect to leave; they only experience a slow decay into further irrelevance and inconsequence. They are unwanted, unlovely, unvalued. They do not expect to be claimed by anybody.

Many of those who end up on the scrap-heap of life are victims of Satan's clever ploys. His luring promises are quite tempting: for recognition, importance, wealth, acceptance. But Satan's only intention is to deposit us on that very same scrap-heap. Satan is the accuser – we cannot trust his promises; we cannot believe his designs. Many of us who are ensnared by his devious wiles notice far too late that we bear a sign round our neck which reads, 'Sold for scrap'.

Simon Peter may well have felt the weight of that same sign around his neck at that breakfast on the beach. Despite his initial personal encounter with Jesus, I imagine that memories of his threefold failure still weighed heavily on him. His mind was still processing all that was happening. He must have wondered if there was any scope for him in the future. Perhaps he had counted himself out of the running for that leadership position in the Church which Jesus had promised him. After all, having denied your master three times in one night, there's not much chance of a second chance, is there?

But for the man of the threefold denial was another man with a threefold reinstatement plan. Peter was to discover that for every mistake he had made, there was a fresh grace to be given; for every time he had fallen, there was a hand to lift him up.

For each time he had spoken in denial of Jesus, he was given the opportunity to speak in love. And in so doing, Peter discovered that the grace of Jesus was amply sufficient to meet his inadequacy. For the paradox of the cross is that it is the antidote of all the horrifying things with which we associate it:

- The cross looked like a failure – yet it is the key which unlocks the door of the losers' prison.
- The cross was a picture of pain – yet by the wounds of Jesus we find healing.
- The cross symbolized abandonment by God – yet it stands as the ultimate peace treaty for those who welcome its authority.

Maybe you feel like Peter did – as if you've been left on that scrap-heap to rust. You feel the weight of that 'Sold for scrap' sign around your neck. You think no one will ever come for you now. You can't believe you'll ever be of any future use in the Kingdom. You say of yourself, 'Look at me! No one would want me now – least of all God. I'm no use to anyone.'

Let the story of Peter encourage you. Jesus not only gave Peter back his dignity; he also gave him back his job. 'Feed my lambs,' said Jesus. 'Take care of my sheep. I said I would build my Church on you. Your failure does not set aside my intentions; they still apply to the one who restates their love for me, just as you have done.'

The same gift of grace is offered to us also. We may feel sorrow for our failure; we may feel our life is a mess and that we are no longer presentable, least of all to God. Yet Jesus says, 'That's just why I came'.

By his death and resurrection Jesus can remove that 'Sold for scrap' sign and replace it with a medal around your neck, the inscription on which reads, 'Reclaimed by love'. When the world thinks you're only fit to rust, God declares you're worth reclaiming. When Satan challenges your usefulness, God proclaims your unique potential.

Martin Luther captured this wonderful reclaimable work of God in the following words: 'Our God knows how to ride the lame horse and carve the rotten wood'. Carving rotten wood – yes, God is very good at that – in fact, he's had plenty of training, his skills most finely honed while being a carpenter in Nazareth in the early first century.

For further reflection

1 Acknowledge before God an area of your life where you feel you have failed. Bring it to the cross where Jesus died to set you free from that failure. Ask God to give you a fresh start. Be open to how the Lord may wish to lead you on from this.

2 Pray for someone you know who is conscious of failure. Ask God to draw close to them to lift them up. How could you help them at this time?

A prayer

Lord, I was a sinner, but you died for me.
I was guilty, but you took the blame.
I was unacceptable, but you chose me.
I was broken, but you've begun to mend me.
I was empty, and yet you've filled me.
I was sold for scrap, and yet you've reclaimed me through your death on the cross.
Lord, I praise you for your love.

Day 32 (Wednesday)

❧

A spiritual check-up

'Simon, son of John, do you truly love me more than these?'

(John 21.15)

When Jesus asked Peter three times if he loved him, he was, as ever, getting at the heart of the matter. For his questions were ones of devotion and loyalty. Where betrayal had taken place, allegiance had to be sworn. It was only natural for Jesus to question Peter in this way: failure had struck and old habits had begun to reappear, so Jesus had every right to quiz Peter about the extent of his commitment. It was time to check that the man who had been derailed was coming back on track.

In many ways Jesus was giving Peter a spiritual check-up. He was probing to the roots of his commitment, searching for the true objects of his devotion. In many types of job, regular medicals are obligatory for staff as a way of ensuring that they are in peak condition. How important do we consider spiritual check-ups? What is the state of our spiritual health? Christians are generally poor at having spiritual check-ups. I believe this is part of the mentality I mentioned on Day 22, whereby this is a taboo subject generally among Christians. Yet spiritual health is vital in order for us effectively to share the good news.

So, let's undergo a quick check-up today. It's our turn now – we're in the hands of the great physician.

First he takes our temperature. What is our spiritual temperature like at the moment? It was Jesus who accused the Laodicean church of being neither hot nor cold (Revelation 3.16). Spiritual lukewarmness is a common malaise. It's like the common cold of the soul. To what extent can we speak of having a vibrant, warm faith?

Next he takes our pulse. What is the rhythm of our life like? Does it beat to God's tune or one which we have made?

Now he checks our breathing. It has been said that prayer is to the soul what breath is to the body – in other words, rather important. How is our prayer-life? Do we struggle in short spurts, with much coughing and spluttering? Are we simply short of breath?

Next it's time to check our reflexes and responses. How do we respond to God and his requirements? Does he get much reaction from us? Being determined to do God's will may involve us doing many things for him. Are we sluggish in how we view his authority? What is the extent of our obedience?

So how well do we think we did? The above exercises are not designed to give the whole picture of our spiritual health, but will certainly provide some general indications. More important, how satisfied do we think the great physician is with our check-up? What will be the doctor's verdict? Will he choose to highlight anything in particular that gave cause for concern?

Jesus was pleased with the results of Peter's check-up. It revealed a man who clearly desired a fresh start and was eager to restate the depth of his own commitment. Peter was humble enough to accept this unannounced check-up, and his words reveal his submission to the one who knew better than anyone else how to identify the state of his spiritual fitness: '"Lord, you know all things; you know that I love you."'

Check-ups like this are very personal; we can feel as if we've been put under the spotlight. It's easy to try and avoid the issue, or change the subject. Peter was a little too intrigued about John's future: '"What is that to you? You must follow me."' Jesus was telling him not to worry about other people, but to allow the focus of his attention to be on himself. A spiritual check-up means that we must allow the Lord to search us freely, and reveal the things that would prevent us from following him more closely. We should allow this to happen as regularly as we can.

For further reflection

1 Go through the above section again slowly, giving as much time as you can to thinking through your answers to the questions raised about our prayer life, spiritual temperature, obedience and rhythm of life.

2 If you feel unfit in any particular area of your spiritual life, ask the Lord to show you the reasons why this may be so. Resolve to do something practical to help – for example, read a book on the subject, or talk to your minister or a mature Christian and seek their counsel.

A prayer

Father, you are the great physician.
Help me to stay fit.
Protect my spiritual health and the disciplines which seek to maintain it.
May your Spirit within me regulate my life rhythm,
until my heart beats always in time with yours.
For Jesus' sake. Amen.

Final Instructions

Then the eleven disciples went to Galilee, to the mountain where Jesus had told them to go. When they saw him, they worshipped him; but some doubted. Then Jesus came to them and said, 'All authority in heaven and on earth has been given to me. Therefore go and make disciples of all nations, baptizing them in the name of the Father and of the Son and of the Holy Spirit, and teaching them to obey everything I have commanded you. And surely I will be with you always, to the very end of the age.'

(Matthew 28.16–20)

'You are witnesses of these things. I am going to send you what my Father has promised; but stay in the city until you have been clothed with power from on high.'

(Luke 24.48–9)

'But you will receive power when the Holy Spirit comes on you; and you will be my witnesses in Jerusalem, and in all Judea and Samaria, and to the ends of the earth.'

(Acts 1.8)

Day 33 (Thursday)

❧

The great commission

'Therefore go and make disciples of all nations, baptizing them in the name of the Father and of the Son and of the Holy Spirit, and teaching them to obey everything I have commanded you.'

(Matthew 28.19–20)

We have arrived at the very crux of Jesus' plan to send out the disciples with his good news. So far we have seen him appear in various ways to provide convincing proof of his resurrection. He has dealt with the fears and doubts which had plagued the disciples following the horrifying events of Good Friday. In his latest appearances he has been beginning to talk about sending them out to do his work, introducing his plan for the disciples. Now he explains in a nutshell the full scope of what has been called 'the great commission'.

'Go and make disciples of all nations' has become one of the most quoted of Jesus' commands, especially during the 1990s, which have been called the Decade of Evangelism. Jesus gave this command 2,000 years ago – and every decade since then has been an opportunity to obey that command. In recent years it has been encouraging to see Jesus' call to action becoming a high priority for many churches. I long to see this in every church in our land.

That God should choose us to be the channels through which he reveals himself to the world is remarkable, for God has no need of anyone's help to achieve his purposes. He is fully self-sufficient; he is separate from, and can exist without, everything he has created. Yet he chooses people of his own making to be the agents of his salvation in the world. Most of us would argue that God would do a far better job without us – but that is not his style. His way is one of relationship, choosing to reveal himself through the lives of those who wish to be his people.

There is nothing to compare with this plan of campaign. Artists may choose to express themselves through, for example, a piece of sculpture – their creation is inanimate, and its life and message is derived solely from the interpretation placed upon it by those who view it.

How different it is with God, the divine sculptor. He has created us as people and breathed his life into us. And those who follow him have his eternal life through the power of his Holy Spirit within them. God therefore expresses himself through us, living in us. He has made his home in us, just as Jesus said he would (John 14.23).

The great commission involves three aspects of people being brought to faith. The first is the actual act of someone's conversion – the making of a disciple. Then there is baptism – a sign of the new life they have received in Christ. Thirdly there is receiving instruction in the Christian life – the process of coming to maturity as a believer. All three stages are important. Sadly many of us have become too interested in the first stage. We strive only to make converts, forgetting that what follows is vital for the long-term survival of their faith. Our aim is to make disciples for life. New-born babies do not grow on their own; they need proper care and feeding. New-born believers need a similar standard of care to ensure that they grow up in their faith.

The great commission tends to highlight the depth of our own commitment to following him. We have seen in recent days how Jesus' reinstatement of Peter involved a fresh declaration of Peter's love for his Lord. We see in Matthew's Gospel a further testing of the disciples' commitment, as he calls them to action. As Jesus approached them on that Galilean mountainside to give them this command, we are told that there were still doubts among some of them. The Greek word *distazō*, used here for doubt, is worth commenting on: it is only used twice in the whole New Testament, both times by Matthew. It implies a twofold dilemma, an uncertainty over a choice of two different directions. The other occurrence of this word is found in Matthew 14.31, when Peter is chastised by Jesus for his lack of faith while walking on the water. Both occasions were moments of critical decision. Peter was unsure which way to go in the middle of the storm: back to the boat, or press on to Jesus? And the disciples on that Galilean hillside were pressed towards a similar choice: to believe that Jesus really was who he said he was and spread his gospel, or to turn back from following him?

Here lies the heart of the matter: there is a world which needs the good news of Jesus. We are his agents. There is an old legend that tells of Jesus' return to heaven. On his arrival there, the angels quiz him about his future plans. 'I have left eleven men and a few others to continue the work,' he told them. 'But what if they don't succeed?' asked the angels. 'I have no further plans,' came the reply.

We are the bearers of good tidings. We have a divine appointment to be God's mouthpiece. He has chosen no other way of revealing himself now to the human race. Only if we play our part can we together give a full picture of the God whose love we should long to share.

For further reflection

1 What is your reaction to the great commission? Perhaps you have been put off sharing your faith because of bad experiences in the past, or because you have witnessed bad models of evangelism. Do you find that you are in a dilemma about whether to risk stepping out in faith for God? Bring your own fears to the Lord. Spend some time acknowledging your position before him, and then pray that he would begin his work of changing your heart and mind to trust him more. Praise him that he has chosen to use you to reveal himself to other people.

2 How could you seek to be available to God in the light of today's reading? Turn your thoughts into prayer.

A prayer

Here I am, Lord.

I want to be ready to speak for you.

Forgive me for the times when I'm not much of an advert for your good news.

I feel so weak and helpless sometimes.

But your grace is stronger still,

and has brought me further than I would have dared to believe.

That's a story in itself.

Help me to share it with others,

so that they can become members of your family. Amen.

Day 34 (Friday)

✿

With a story to tell

'You are witnesses of these things.'
(Luke 24.48)

It had been quite a day. You had awoken that morning to
the darkness to which your blindness had confined you
since birth. You had taken up your customary begging
position in the hope that today would somehow be better
than the rest of the week. Precious few coins had fallen in
your bowl recently. Identifying compassionate passers-by
was a difficult job when you were blind. Yes, you'd really
hoped it would be a better day. You never imagined that,
by evening, you'd be able to see. And that was all because
of Jesus healing you.

It seemed like the best news in the world. But things
had got unpleasant when you started telling your family
and friends. All you did was tell the story. OK, the spit-
and-make-mud-pies-on-the-face episode was a little
strange – but more bizarre still was that some of your
nearest and dearest seemed to forget who you were. Surely
having two good eyes doesn't make you look that different, does it?

And why did those Pharisees have to get involved?
Things only got worse when they questioned you – the
same interrogation as with your friends. All you could do
was tell your story like it happened. But they didn't want
to listen to you. So in came your parents, but they didn't
really stick up for you either. They just wanted to keep on
the right side of the Pharisees.

Questions, questions, so many questions. You weren't
educated enough to answer them fully, so you just told

129

your story. You weren't clever enough to see through their schemes, so you just told your story. You didn't know everything about Jesus, so you just told your story. And the gist of it was simple: '"One thing I do know. I was blind, but now I see"' (John 9.25).

The story of the man born blind in John 9 illustrates perfectly what it means to be a witness. This is one of the descriptions applied by Jesus to how we can obey his call to action. In a court of law the evidence of a witness can dramatically alter the whole course of a trial – many of us have seen court dramas on TV where the unexpected arrival of a new witness turns the tables on all that has gone before. Witnesses play a key role.

The Greek word for witness is *martus* (from which the word martyr comes), which denotes someone who is able to speak, or who does speak, of what they have seen and heard. I find great encouragement from the fact that the use of *martus* implies that we all possess the ability to convey what we have experienced. When Jesus said we would be his witnesses, he was assuring us that we all have a story to tell. For that is what being a witness is all about. We don't have to be clever speakers with extroverted personalities – we just have to speak of what we have seen and heard.

The early disciples took up the challenge of being witnesses for Jesus. They ended up under cross-examination, just like the man born blind. On one occasion Peter and John found themselves being scrutinized by the Sanhedrin (the Jewish high court) when they were preaching and teaching. When charged not to speak about Jesus, their response was unequivocal: '"We cannot help speaking about what we have seen and heard"' (Acts 4.20). Peter and John were uneducated men: they had not attended theological college; they were not trained preachers. The main thing which qualified them as witnesses was that they had spent time with Jesus. This was what most profoundly struck the Sanhedrin (Acts 4.13).

We do not have to know everything about Christianity to be a witness for Christ. There will be many things we may not understand. But don't let what you don't know damage what you do know. Our own experiences are a powerful tool when it comes to playing our part in Jesus' call to action. Personal testimony is one of the most effective means of sharing our faith. It does not rely on intellect or theological training – we are simply telling our story. When we share something of what God has done for us, we are showing the practical relevance of our faith which is grounded in real life.

The great promise of Jesus is that he will give us the words to say when it comes to speaking for him (see Luke 12.12). One thing we always have is our own story. People may try to cut us down with clever arguments; they may seek to shoot down our faith with brash words. But in the midst of this battle, one banner may always be flown: that of our own testimony. God will deal with each of us as individuals, but all of us can echo the words of the man born blind: "'One thing I do know. I was blind, but now I see.'" For us the blindness may have been spiritual rather than physical – God's work in bringing either spiritual understanding or physical sight is nothing short of a grace-filled miracle. Let's be a storyteller among the people we know.

For further reflection

Jot down some thoughts under the following headings:

- What my life was like before I became a Christian.
- How it was that I became a Christian.
- How my faith has helped me since then.

These thoughts are a synopsis of your own story of faith. What, if anything, makes it difficult for you to speak of these things? Ask God to give you strength, courage and opportunities to share your story with others.

A prayer of praise

Amazing grace! how sweet the sound
That saved a wretch like me!
I once was lost, but now am found,
Was blind, but now I see.

(John Newton, 1725–1807)

Day 35 (Saturday)

※

Worshippers before witnesses

When they saw him, they worshipped him.
(Matthew 20.17)

I can well remember my excitement when I first began to realize my own calling to go and share the good news of Jesus with those around me. I used to pray for what I can only describe as golden opportunities to explain the Christian faith to others. What I mean by that is the hit-me-right-between-the-eyes situation when someone comes up to you and asks, quite out of the blue, 'How do I become a Christian?' It is the ultimate opening to share your faith. It's served straight up for you, all beautifully presented without any of the fuss of having to try and bring about a preliminary conversation.

I soon discovered that such opportunities were, for me at least, few and far between. In fact, I think this has only happened to me once in the 14 years I have been a Christian. What I have learned over this time is not that God cannot bring about such occurrences, but rather that evangelism is a process, and that all those who come to faith do so through a journey that is often gradual and always unique. It is also true that to engage in evangelism is not to wait for these dramatic events, but to live daily in the power of God's Spirit in a way that makes the gospel attractive to those whom we meet.

I was intrigued to discover how the early apostles coped with their first forays into the world with the good news of Jesus. And I was even more fascinated to see whether any of those golden opportunities were presented to them for which I longed – and still do. A study of the book of Acts reveals two events of this nature which I would like to highlight, because they each reveal an important prerequisite for all those who seek to share the Gospel.

The first comes on the Day of Pentecost itself. Following the gift of the Holy Spirit to the believers, Peter preaches his first post-resurrection public sermon. Notice the response of those who heard: '"Brothers, what shall we do?"' (Acts 2.37). An open door was presented to the apostles as the people were 'cut to the heart' – 3,000 people found faith that day.

The second event comes later, in Acts 16. Here the circumstances are very different. Paul and Silas have no crowds hanging on their every word, no glorious surroundings of Jerusalem. God was unmistakeably present on the Day of Pentecost – but Paul and Silas were in a place which most people would have described as God-forsaken: the dungeons of Philippi. It had been a bad day for them, all in all: they had cast an evil spirit from a slave-girl and ended up seized, dragged away, stripped, beaten and imprisoned.

But suddenly God brings the house down, literally. The ground shook, the walls shook, the prisoners shook, their chains shook off, the lights shook out and the jailer was so shook up at thinking he'd lost all his inmates that he went to kill himself. A quick intervention from Paul assured the jailer that no one was missing. And what did all this lead to? Another golden opportunity – for the jailer asks the question: '"Sirs, what must I do to be saved?"' (Acts 16.30). You can't be presented with a clearer opportunity than that.

On reflection, it struck me how both these incidents involved a preliminary aspect of worship. On the Day of Pentecost, the gift of the Holy Spirit enabled the apostles, through the gift of tongues, to glorify God in the languages of all the visitors to Jerusalem at that time (Acts 2.11). And Paul and Silas sang songs of praise even while in the dungeon (Acts 16.25). There is a principle here which is good to underline: we cannot be witnesses before we are worshippers. This pattern was established early in the lives of the first disciples. Both Matthew and Luke record that worship was taking place regularly during those 40 days of preparation for mission (Matthew 28.17, Luke 24.53).

It is as we worship that we put down strong roots into the rich soil of God's life. In that soil we are nourished, replenished and strengthened. Such an environment, which draws us close to the Lord, will naturally produce the fruit of service to him.

Worship is chiefly directed to God for who he is; it is therefore independent of our own personal circumstances. It is good to cultivate an attitude of worship to the Lord in all situations. For the God of blessing at Pentecost is the same God who meets us in the dungeon and grants us release. And if we seek to be effective in sharing our faith in all circumstances, we must be those who choose to worship in those same situations also.

I still pray for those golden opportunities to come along. And in our present climate where we see a growing spiritual hunger, may God grant that more such events take place. Hungry people will go to any lengths to get the food they need. But if someone came to us for the bread of life, would we have fed on Jesus enough ourselves, through worship, to have anything to offer them?

For further reflection

1 Spend some time giving thanks and praise to God for who he is and what he has done. Thank him in particular for anything new you have learned since using this book.

2 Cultivate the habit of giving praise to God throughout each day. For someone who worships in different settings will become a witness in them also.

A prayer

Almighty God, I give you praise.
There is none like you.
You never change, though circumstances ceaselessly fluctuate.
Dependable God, I worship you.
Give me a heart to praise you daily.
For your glory alone. Amen.

The Ascension

After he said this, he was taken up before their very eyes, and a cloud hid him from their sight.

They were looking intently up into the sky as he was going, when suddenly two men dressed in white stood beside them. 'Men of Galilee,' they said, 'why do you stand here looking into the sky? This same Jesus, who has been taken from you into heaven, will come back in the same way you have seen him go into heaven.'

(Acts 1.9–11)

And God raised us up with Christ and seated us with him in the heavenly realms in Christ Jesus.

(Ephesians 2.6)

Christ Jesus is at the right hand of God and is also interceding for us.

(Romans 8.34)

Day 36 (Sunday)

Join the victory parade

> But thanks be to God who always leads us in triumphal
> procession in Christ.
>
> (2 Corinthians 2.14)

Our 40-day journey with the first disciples is approaching
its end. In our final section we will focus on the ascension
of Jesus and its significance within God's plan of calling us
to action.

Of all the events which took place in the life of Christ,
his ascension is probably the least regarded. We marvel at
his humble birth, are astonished by his miracles, stand in
awe of the cross and applaud his resurrection. But when it
comes to the ascension, we are not nearly so moved.
Ascension Day (being a Thursday) is one of the most fre-
quently missed days in the Church's year.

Far from being an event full of anticlimax after all that
has gone before, the ascension of Jesus is, I believe, the
perfect seal upon his whole earthly ministry. Each event in
his life had a proper place and purpose, and was entirely
essential to the whole plan of salvation. There would have
been no point in the cross without the resurrection. There
would have been no point in the resurrection without the
ascension.

The return of Jesus to his rightful place in heaven was
the final sign and seal on everything he had accomplished
on earth. In the terminology of the Olympic Games, if the
resurrection was his actual crossing of the line to win the
gold medal, the ascension was the presentation ceremony
for that medal with a heavenly anthem heralding his
triumph.

The return of Jesus to heaven is described by the writer to the Hebrews, who casts Jesus in the role of a great high priest presenting the ultimate sacrifice to atone for the sins of the world – himself. And the Father has looked upon this offering with favour (Hebrews 10.12–14). In recognition of the success of his earthly mission, Jesus is accorded the highest place of honour at the right hand of the Father. He laid aside all vestiges of glory when he left heaven to live upon earth; following the ascension he received it all back again. In his vision in Revelation, St John describes the victory ceremony Jesus received on returning to heaven. Countless angels join their voices in a chorus of adoration: '"Worthy is the Lamb who was slain, to receive power and wealth and wisdom and strength and honour and glory and praise!"' (Revelation 5.12).

When a football team has won the FA Cup, they often drive through their city in an open-top bus, proudly showing off the trophy to cheering fans who line the streets. No victory parade on earth has come close to the reception Jesus was given on his return to heaven. His sacrifice had been accepted; salvation for all people who believe had been secured. Heaven has always provided the best facilities for celebrations, and the heavenly host came out in strength to make this an occasion not to be missed. What a homecoming!

The most wonderful thing about this victory procession is that it has not just been confined to the courts of heaven. Jesus is leading us all in his parade of triumph: 'But thanks be to God who always leads us in triumphal procession in Christ and through us spreads everywhere the fragrance of the knowledge of him' (2 Corinthians 2.14).

What a fantastic picture Paul gives us here. Down all the years since that first Easter, Jesus has been calling his people to join his parade of victory. It's like the longest conga ever danced – one believer beckons to another, 'Come on! Join the dance!' And so the procession continues down the years, across the boundaries of age and race, across the divisions of nation and colour.

But notice that this procession is not just for us. It is one of fragrance for those who stand and watch. For there are many who are not part of the parade. They line the streets and look on; there are others who do not even know there's a procession going on. Ours is a celebration designed to touch the hearts of all those on the side-lines. Paul says we are like fragrance; through us, God is wanting to kiss a broken and hurting world in love. And as we draw near to those in need of his life, so his fragrance wafts gently over them, allowing them to breathe in the aroma of Christ.

The victory procession of Christ is one of the most beautiful images in the Bible of how we view our mission of sharing his good news. It all began at the ascension.

Christ has achieved his victory; all is accomplished. And his reward? Is it not us, the people he has ransomed? He has won a people for himself. And we, in that marvellous procession, respond in return with our praise and thanksgiving.

For further reflection

1 Join in the victory parade today by praising Jesus for his triumph. If you are able to attend church today, enjoy the fellowship of the other members of the congregation. Together you are all part of the victory parade.

2 Think about how fragrance is used. How could you be fragrance this week for Christ?

A prayer

Lord Jesus, I celebrate your victory:
You have conquered death,
and have ascended to the highest place in heaven.
Lead me to dance in your victory procession,
proclaiming the good news you have given to us.
Suffuse me with the aroma of Christ,
that I may be your fragrance everywhere I go.
For Jesus' sake. Amen.

Day 37 (Monday)

❧

Come up to a better seat

And God raised us up with Christ.
(Ephesians 2.6)

We continue to discover more of the significance of the ascension, today focusing on the position of authority which Jesus holds now that he has returned to his Father.

In heaven there is a place at the Father's right hand. The one who occupies it has the authority, power and favour of the Father. That place is reserved for Christ alone. It has always been reserved for him; for all eternity it has only ever had his name on it. No other being, angelic or otherwise, has ever been offered this position by the Father's side.

The Bible is very clear about the extent of the authority accorded to Jesus: '[Jesus is] ... far above all rule and authority, power and dominion and every title that can be given, not only in this age, but also in the one to come' (Ephesians 1.21). '[Jesus has] gone into heaven and is at God's right hand – with angels, authorities and powers in submission to him' (1 Peter 3.22).

I love that phrase in Ephesians: 'above ... every title that can be given'. Think of all the merits and awards we give to those who are born into a position, or who achieve something great. As I am writing this chapter, the Queen's New Year's honours list has just been published. The newspapers are full of all kinds of personalities newly bearing MBEs, OBEs, life peerages and the like. We honour the intelligent with doctorates, the athletic with Olympic gold medals, the gallant with the VC, the peace-makers with the Nobel Prize, film stars with Oscars. But no human honour comes close to the position which Jesus holds at the right hand of the Father. It is absolutely without parallel. We could never dream up an award great enough to measure fully the merit of Christ. He is above every title we could ever create.

The wonder of the gospel is that out of his love for us, Jesus, for a brief time, set aside that position of glory which is too great to define. In Philippians we are told that he 'made himself nothing, taking the very nature of a servant, being made in human likeness' (Philippians 2.7). You can't get much more of a contrast than that! Through the events of that first Easter he purchased our freedom from sin. In recognition of his triumph, he took back his rightful place at the Father's side: 'God exalted him to the highest place' (Philippians 2.9).

What a position of privilege and power. In fact, long ago, it became all too tempting for someone who would pay a high price for trying to seize it. That special position became the battleground over which Satan fought for ascendancy in heaven. He desired to have that special place and sought by force to attain it. He was defeated and he and his minions were cast down out of heaven and since then have been active in seeking to usurp God's rule (see Isaiah 14.12–15; Ezekiel 28.12–17).

The ascension of Jesus was the reverse of Satan's fall from heaven. Satan lost his position of authority, and his followers also fell, taking the same punishment as their leader. One of the most amazing things about the ascension is that, just as Jesus was lifted up back to his rightful place of power, so the Father invites us to be lifted up to sit with his son: 'And God raised us up with Christ and seated us with him in the heavenly realms in Christ Jesus' (Ephesians 2.6).

This is quite an invitation – to sit with Jesus in that most privileged of places. It's like sitting with the Queen in the royal box at a great public performance. The royal box has the finest seats with the best view – you get all the royal benefits. Perhaps you feel that life has given you a raw deal, that you have been relegated to the back row. Your seat is lumpy and uncomfortable due to restricted leg-room; the view is terrible as you are so far away; the acoustics are not good, either. How you long for a better seat!

Because of the ascension, your yearning can be fulfilled. The Father is beckoning to us from his position: 'Come on up and join us here! Come and have a better place! Sit with us!' God always gives the best invitations. Don't let this one pass you by.

For further reflection

1 Give praise to the Lord for who he is – he has the name above every name.

2 Ask the Lord to help you grasp the fact that *you* are seated with Christ 'in the heavenly realms'. Ask him to help you resist the Devil who seeks to prevent us from recognizing our identity and position in Christ.

A prayer of praise

Now you are exalted to the highest place,
King of the heavens, where one day I'll bow.
But for now, I marvel at this saving grace.
I'm full of praise once again.

Day 38 (Tuesday)

The one who pleads our cause

Christ Jesus ... is at the right hand of God and is also interceding for us.

(Romans 8.34)

I like a good courtroom drama. The questioning, the counter-arguments, the clever advocacy of the barristers – all combine for an enthralling scene. The need for justice to prevail comes through strongly. Sometimes real-life court cases make the headlines, particularly ones which go to the high court for a final ruling.

There is one court, however, which never makes the headlines, but which stands higher than any other court in the land: it is the court of heaven, where the world's most righteous judge presides. Imagine that you or I were in the dock. I hate to say this, but things don't look too good for us – the case against us looks very black indeed. In fact, the evidence against us is utterly convincing. We have all fallen short; we have all transgressed the laws of God; we have gone our own way and failed to follow our creator. In short, we are guilty. And there we stand in the dock, already convicted, awaiting the just judgement which we deserve.

But who is this who rises to defend us? An advocate has come to plead for us before the judge of all. He is not only a passionate advocate, he is sympathetic too. As he begins to argue our case, we realize he has been subject to all our human limitations. He has been tired, misunderstood and frustrated; he has been angered and troubled in spirit. But he did not cave in under any of these pressures. And in that strength of understanding he has prepared our defence.

Who is our defender? It is Jesus, who took up our cause even before we were personally aware of our guilt. In that passage from Romans, Paul reminds us that Jesus is 'at the right hand of the Father and is also interceding for us' (Romans 8.34).

This is a most incredible thing. Jesus is pleading our cause in the highest court in the whole universe. He upholds our cause, declaring to all that judgement and punishment have already been carried out – on him, no less. Vengeance against sin has been fully satisfied. Through his own death and resurrection, God's righteous justice has been administered. Jesus, the sinless one, has taken all the blame: 'After he had provided purification for sins, he sat down at the right hand of the Majesty in heaven' (Hebrews 1.3).

Jesus' work that first Easter was a complete success. He now holds the finest argument for our acquittal – it is a totally watertight case. He has already paid the penalty. There is nothing more to pay. The case against us collapses; the jury is dismissed.

And now there is no one left to condemn us. It reminds me of the story of the woman caught in adultery who was brought before Jesus (John 8.1–11). Her accusers wanted her blood: Jesus instead gave mercy, knowing that his blood would fully pay off her guilt. Her accusers wanted swift condemnation – the Pharisees had written off that woman. Jesus instead simply wrote in the dust; he did not condone her sin, but revealed the sin in the lives of those who cried for vengeance.

And by the time he straightened up, the accusers had melted away. When Jesus defends us, the accusations against us cannot stand alongside him. Just as the older Pharisees left the scene first, so those long-standing accusations levelled at us start to fall away when Jesus takes up our case. We need not fear them anymore. Harmful charges – true and untrue – made against us years ago can melt away when we allow Jesus to plead for us.

So finally, at the end of our trial, we stand, like that woman, without any accusers. And we hear our advocate's words, 'Has no one condemned you?' With assurance we can look around us and say, 'No one, sir'.

And then come six words of exquisite grace which only the Saviour of the world could speak: 'Then neither do I condemn you'. What a declaration of innocence! And if he will not condemn us, no one else can bring a charge either. To go beyond Easter is to live a life free from condemnation. Remember that our advocate is always upholding our cause, and in that assurance we can go out in his strength to serve him in the world.

For further reflection

1 Worship Jesus for his saving power, that his death on the cross frees us from all sin.

2 Do you feel guilty about any particular issue in your life at the moment? Remember that Jesus promises to defend our cause if we are repentant and seek his Kingdom. What sort of things do you think he would say to uphold justice for you? Invite him into your situation. Ask him to give you his perspective.

A prayer

Vindicate me, O Lord.
Strengthen me to live a blameless life,
trusting in you without wavering.
Test me and try me; examine my heart and mind.
Lead me to walk continually in your truth.
Do not let me sit with the deceitful and evil,
but let me instead proclaim your praise
and tell of your wonderful deeds.
Place my feet on level ground.
For your glory's sake. Amen.
(Based on Psalm 26)

Day 39 (Wednesday)

❧❧❧

Don't just stand there!

'Why do you stand here looking into the sky?'
(Acts 1.11)

Over the past six weeks we have encountered many
deeply searching questions which were asked of the first
disciples. We have overheard the angels at the empty tomb
rebuking the women for seeking the living among the
dead. We have listened to the compassionate voice of the
risen Christ in the garden that morning asking Mary why
she was crying. We have heard his question go over the
water to the disciples after their unsuccessful fishing expe-
dition, challenging them about their fruitless labours.

Today I would like us to focus our attention on one
further searching question. It comes to the disciples as they
strain their eyes for a final glimpse of Jesus as he is taken
from them. But he had already gone. While gazing at the
heavens, they missed the two angels who had appeared
right beside them on the earth. Their question exposed
this fact: "'Why do you stand here looking into the sky?'"

This question underlined the urgency of the mission
the disciples were being required to undertake. In our day,
with an ever-increasing population straining the earth's
resources, the task of bringing the gospel to all nations is
more demanding still. Sadly the Western Church does not
seem to have fully grasped the enormity of the job at
hand. In a world where four people die every second, it is
estimated that it takes 1,000 Christians 365 days to bring
one new person to faith in Christ. I'll let you do the maths
on this, but one thing is clear from these figures – this is
not good enough.

In the Church we have developed great expertise in analysing our structures, meetings and buildings. We form sub-groups from our committees for what we trust will be even greater effectiveness. We spend hours discussing the minutiae of church life. In no way do I wish to criticize any church's pursuit of excellence. I think we are not always good at evaluating all that takes place in the Church. The danger I wish to highlight is simply that we can fall prey to prolonged navel-gazing which takes our eyes off the very aim of our task. Listen to some of Jesus' words: '"Do you not say, 'Four months more and then the harvest'? I tell you, open your eyes and look at the fields! They are ripe for harvest"' (John 4.35).

Jesus gives us a clear picture of the urgency and imme-diacy of the task. The fields are ready for harvest. So often our mentality can be one of 'four months more and then the harvest'. We think we'll just wait a bit more; we are those who often put things off until another time. In con-trast, Jesus showed us that the harvest is plentiful but the workers are few. This is what makes the task urgent. The issue seems to be not so much about the size of the poten-tial workforce; after all, there are plenty of Christians around. What is lacking is those from the workforce who are actively labouring in the harvest-fields.

One problem is our view of what constitutes the harvest-fields. The idea of missionary work is often limited to foreign countries, and we can therefore form the opinion that these are the places, these are the kind of workers, which Jesus means. However, when Jesus told us to look at the readiness of the fields for harvest, he did not necessarily expect us to be looking with long-range vision: our neighbourhood, our street, our very homes, are just as much places of harvest as any other. God cannot give us the nations until our hearts are also moved with compassion for the communities around us. These are entrusted to us also. Genuine concern for the world must be rooted consistently in a concern for our locality.

Peter, who preached the momentous first post-resurrection sermon on the Day of Pentecost, knew well the urgency of Jesus' call to action: 'Always be ready to give an answer for the hope you have' (1 Peter 3.15). Notice the word 'always'. Not sometimes, not when we feel good about the day, not just when we like the person we're talking to – we are always to be ready. This is not an option that we may select every third Tuesday of the month. When it comes to the harvest, when it's ready, it's ready. If what is ripe for harvest is just left, it goes to seed and is lost. You have to act when the fields are ready.

Jesus has surveyed the fields and his verdict is that they are ripe. If we are to trust his assessment of the scene, it will surely spur us on to action. 'Now is the time of God's favour, now is the day of salvation' (Hebrews 6.2b).

For further reflection

1 Examine your own reaction to Jesus' words in John 4.35. Confess any attitude that has relegated the great commission to a place of low priority in your life.

2 What constitutes the harvest fields near you? What practically could you do to build bridges with others in these places, and so seek to share the good news with them?

A prayer

Lord Jesus, I see the fields
and I hear your words about the harvest.
I do not want to shrink from the task.
Make me a labourer, Lord;
the fields are all about me.
I want to share in the work of the harvest.
You know all about me and the way you can use me.
Lord, there is a task to undertake.
I am as ready to reap as the fields are for harvest.
Here I am, available for work. Amen.

Day 40
(Ascension Day – Thursday)

――――――― ✤ ―――――――

The best promise of all

'I will be with you always, to the very end of the age.'
(Matthew 28.20)

Jesus must be the only person who celebrated his own departure from the earth, saying it was good for all who loved him (see John 16.7). In the normal course of events, a loss such as this would be tragic for all those left behind. Jesus is the only person to predict a genuine gain through what appeared to be a definite loss. He meant what he said – and all his disciples since then have discovered the truth of those words.

During his earthly ministry, Jesus was subject to his human limitations of space and time – his disciples relied on his physical presence. But the greatest benefit of the ascension is that Jesus now sends his Spirit into our lives so that we may enjoy his presence everywhere. '"Surely I am with you always to the very end of the age"' (Matthew 28.20). It's the best promise of all, that we never have to lose the presence of Christ if we seek to follow him.

It's the promise which should encourage all those who seek to go beyond Easter with the good news of Jesus. The great missionary David Livingstone is one fine example of this. His writings speak of how this promise sustained him during long days of loneliness in Africa as he tirelessly worked for the advancement of the gospel. It's the promise we need if we are to serve the Lord. As we saw in the first week of our readings, he is faithful in keeping his word. He is utterly committed to granting us his presence 'to the very end'. He's not just a short-term God: he is there for the long haul. He doesn't give up on us half-way through – he is whole-heartedly for us, sticking by us to the very end: to the very end of our illness, the very end of our working career, the very end of our tether, the very end of our life. He is there.

God chooses to pursue his relationship with us. Don't you find that Christmas is a good time of year to test the strength of your long-range friendships? One year we may not receive a Christmas card from someone, even though we sent them one. We may decide to give it one more year, but if the same thing happens, we often assume it's time to let that particular friendship lapse.

In contrast, God never lets his relationship with us lapse. And the strength of that commitment is so clearly seen in the best Christmas gift ever given – Jesus. God always gets in touch.

The closeness of his presence which Jesus initiated after his ascension is something he plans to bring to full-ness when he comes back a second time. He said, '"And if I go and prepare a place for you, I will come back and take you to be with me that you also may be where I am"' (John 14.3). Jesus' ascension looks forward to his second coming. The angels said to the disciples after Jesus had ascended: '"This same Jesus, who has been taken from you into heaven, will come back in the same way you have seen him go into heaven"' (Acts 1.11). Jesus left the earth's stage after playing his part there to the full. But a day will come when a great curtain-call and a triumphant encore will welcome him back to that same stage.

The first time he came to earth, he left all his glory behind; the next time it will accompany him. The first time he came in obscurity; the next time, all will see him. The first time he left us behind to work for him on the earth; the next time he will come back for us because our work will be complete. And we will then enjoy the presence of God for all eternity.

So Jesus' promise is just a taster of what things will be like. But the taster we are given is quite a feast in itself!

Our journey beyond Easter with those first disciples comes to a close today. I trust that in these last 40 days you have been able to share that journey, encountering Jesus through Scripture and the work of the Holy Spirit in your life. We leave those disciples with that great promise of Jesus ringing clear. Those words spoken so long ago are meant for us too. I said that our journey is at an end – of course, it ends only with the pages of this book. For the first disciples of Jesus, their greatest adventure was only just beginning as they watched him disappear from their sight. We leave their story just as a whole new chapter was about to open for them.

Isn't that where we began 40 days ago, with the God who is writing new chapters for us? What chapter will it be now for you? However God leads you, he will be right there with you, true to his promise. Just as with his early disciples, he is there to bring you beyond your doubts, fears and disappointments, and beyond your own comfort zone in order to share his good news with a world that desperately needs it. And that's what going beyond Easter is all about.

For further reflection

1 Look back over your journey over the past 40 days. What have been particular highlights for you? What new insights has the Lord given? Can you see any particular ways in which God has helped you to work through issues?

2 What new chapters has God opened up for you? Pray for his Spirit to lead and guide you forward. Spend some time giving praise to the God of Easter.

A prayer

Lord, I am ready to go beyond Easter.
I desire to live for you; I commit myself to the next
chapter.
And though the journey is only just beginning,
there's no finer journey to take than the one I take with
you.
Lord, I praise you,
you are risen, ascended, glorified. Amen.

Material for Group Work

This final section contains six outlines for groups based around the post-Easter accounts of the resurrection and ascension. They are designed to complement the 40 days of reflections for individuals – thus someone who is using the daily readings will find fresh material through these group studies.

Due to the diversity of groups, the outlines are simply offered as springboards from which groups may move to other approaches. Please adapt the material in any way to suit your particular group.

Week 1

Contemplating the empty tomb

1 Encourage the group to discuss what the early disciples must have been thinking and feeling after Good Friday. Make a list of single words to sum up what they were experiencing (such as disappointment, fear, etc.).

2 The Gospel accounts of the discovery of the empty tomb are a quartet of personal impressions of that

incredible morning. Each writer highlights what for them were the most important aspects of the events which took place. Splitting the group into four, assign one of the following passages to each subgroup:

- Matthew 28.1–10
- Mark 16.1–8
- Luke 24.1–12
- John 20.1–9

Each subgroup should spend some time writing down the main points of the story as featured by their Gospel writer. Then come back together and discover the common threads contained in all the accounts. Identify as much of the significance of these threads as you can.

3 Allow each group member to share briefly about any word or phrase they have read in their passage which they found particularly interesting or helpful.

4 Easter teaches us about the God of new beginnings, who breathes life into situations which seem like dead-ends. Allow each person to share one situation in their life into which they would like God's renewing power to enter. Now pray for each other.

Week 2

Grief in the garden

1 Read Jesus' words in John 11.25–6. Ask the group to give their responses to these words.

2 Make a list of different life-situations where someone might experience a sense of loss or bereavement.

3 Look at three incidents where Jesus met with those who had suffered loss:

- Luke 7.11–17
- John 11.11–44
- John 20.10–18

Discuss how Jesus feels towards those who are bereaved in each of these incidents, and how he sought to comfort them.

4 Allow each member of the group to share as much as they are able about something or someone they have lost recently. Encourage a wide range of sharing – it might be the death of a partner or friend; it might be the loss of the desire to pray. Drawing on the discussion from (3), pray for each other, that the Lord may meet and comfort each person in their loss, and, where appropriate, restore what has been lost.

Week 3

On a journey to Emmaus

1 Read Luke 24.13–35:

- Encourage the group to identify what Cleopas and his friend were feeling as they walked along the road (for example, refer to verses 14, 17b, 19b–21).
- What did Jesus do to help them recognize him?

- How has God challenged your own views and expectations?

2 Allow each group member to share a recent disappointment, or a hope or dream, that they have. Pray for each other in the light of the Emmaus road story.

3 Consider sharing in an informal fellowship meal of bread and wine, praying that just as Christ was revealed to Cleopas and his friend through the breaking of the bread, so he will be more fully revealed to your group.

Week 4

A breakfast on the beach

1 Read John 21.1–20:
- How do you think the disciples were feeling as they waited by the Sea of Galilee?
- What lessons was Jesus trying to teach them through this episode?

2 Allow each group member to share one incident where they realized the lordship of Jesus. Enjoy listening to one another's stories.

3 Let each group member talk about one area of life where they would like to see progress. Pray for one another, thanking God for what he has done in people's lives, as shared in (2).

Week 5

───────────── ◦§◦ ─────────────

Jesus' call to action

1 Read Matthew 28.16–20, and Acts 1.8. How do people in the group react to the great commission? Encourage some initial discussion about this.

2 In Scripture we are given many different images of what it means to share the good news of Jesus. Think about as many of the following analogies as possible, discussing what they can teach us about sharing our faith:

- salt (Matthew 5.13)
- light (Matthew 5.14–16)
- ambassadors (2 Corinthians 5.20)
- fragrance (2 Corinthians 2.14–16)
- witnesses (Acts 1.8).

3 Allow each group member to talk about someone they know who is not a Christian. Pray together for each of these people to come to faith, and that each member of the group would have more opportunities to share their faith with them.

Week 6

The ascension

1 Encourage some initial discussion on the ascension. What do the group members know about it?

2 Read Acts 1.1–11:

  • How do you think the disciples felt as they watched Jesus ascend?
  • What difference would it have made to the disciples now that Jesus was not physically present? What would have been the advantages and the difficulties?
  • How do we feel about seeking to follow the Lord without his physical presence? What helps us to believe in someone we cannot see?

3 Allow each group member to describe one situation in their life where they particularly need to know God's presence. Pray for one another according to the needs expressed. Pray for the Holy Spirit's power to be at work in each other's lives.